D0252079

DAY HIKES IN THE SANTA FE AREA

Founded in 1892, the Sierra Club works in the United States and other countries to restore the quality of the natural environment and to maintain the integrity of ecosystems. Educating the public to understand and support these objectives is a basic part of the Club's program. All are invited to participate in its activities, which include programs to study, explore, and enjoy wildlands.

DAY HIKES

IN THE

SANTA FE AREA

Fourth Edition

Enlarged and Revised

**By The Santa Fe Group
Of The Sierra Club**

Copyright 1995
by
Santa Fe Group of the Sierra Club
Santa Fe, New Mexico 87501

Illustrations copyright 1990 by Robin Bond
Cover art copyright 1995 by Dorothy Grossman

All rights reserved

ISBN: 0-9616458-2-2

Library of Congress Catalog Card Number: 94-74780

First edition, first printing - 1981
First edition, second printing - 1982
Second edition - 1986
Third edition - 1990
Fourth edition - 1995

Published by the Santa Fe Group
of the Sierra Club
440 Cerrillos Road
Santa Fe, New Mexico 87501

Produced by Sunstone Press/Santa Fe, NM

♻ printed on recycled paper

TABLE OF CONTENTS

ACKNOWLEDGMENTS

The fourth edition of this book was a group effort on the part of many dedicated activists.

First of all, thanks are due to the authors of the individual hikes for sharing their knowledge and love of the outdoors and for accepting with good humor and understanding the revisions made by the editors.

Jana Oyler was the impetus behind the publication of this fourth edition. Without her good humor, organizational abilities, tact, and willingness to spend countless hours typing and editing the hikes as they came to her from the contributors and preparing the book for the printer, this book would not now be in your hands. Her job was made easier by the good work of Linda Zwick on the third edition.

Betsy Fuller, Norma McCallan, and Norbert Sperlich deserve special recognition for their commitment and perseverance in putting the final product together. They, along with Jana Oyler, made the final decisions on content and form and spent many hours editing, brainstorming and proofreading.

For the appearance of the final product, we are indebted to Wes Horner for the sketch maps, to Robin Bond for her line drawings and to Dorothy Grossman for the cover design. Lionel Soracco deserves special thanks for handling the printing arrangements. Jim Smith of Sunstone Press was more than helpful in getting the book put together.

Every hike in this book has been test-hiked by people unfamiliar with the trails. Many thanks go to these "scouts" who checked out the hikes and gave suggestions to update and improve the directions: Lë Adams, Elizabeth Altman, Ann Bancroft, Myles Brown, David Clark, E. J. Evangelos, Betsy Fuller, Anna Heiniger, John Jasper, Art Judd, Julie Montoya King, Allison Leon, Don Lowrie, Norma McCallan, the late Dan Mitchem, the late John Muchmore, Margo Murray, Ed Okun, Jana Oyler, Kathy Perkins, Betsy Reed, Norrine Sanders, Lionel Soracco, Norbert Sperlich, Ingrid Vollnhofer, and Bill and Linda Zwick.

Ann Young first promoted the idea of a trail guide for the Santa Fe area; she, Betsy Fuller, and Bill Chudd were the driving forces behind the first three editions of this book. This fourth edition would not exist without their earlier labors of love.

INTRODUCTION

by
Betsy Fuller

The area around Santa Fe contains a wealth of varied hikes perhaps unequaled by any other place in the state. Access to the 12,000 foot peaks of the Sangre de Cristo Mountains is within an hour's drive of the plaza. Winter walks at elevations of less than 6000 feet are within easy reach when the mountains are too deep in snow to be walked. There are several nationally designated wilderness areas nearby, and the Santa Fe National Forest contains over a million and a half acres of land. Within an hour's drive of Santa Fe you can find five of the seven life zones.

The Santa Fe Group of the Sierra Club has felt the need for a guide to this wealth of wilderness, and this volume describes some of the typical walks that are so close. We have included walks that are classed as easy as well as more difficult ones, and we have tried to give fair representation to the many varied types of terrain that are within easy driving distance of Santa Fe. There are other excellent guides describing trails in Bandelier National Monument and in the Sandia Mountains. Because of these, we have limited the number of hikes described in those two areas to a few representative ones. If those areas appeal to you for future exploration, be sure to refer to the publications listed in the "Suggested Reading" section at the back of the book.

Two printings of the first edition of this book and large printings of the second and third editions have sold out. Rather than reprinting the third edition, the editors decided that a completely revised fourth edition was needed. There are eight new hikes in this edition; several hikes from earlier editions have been rewritten.

The money earned from the sales of the book has been used in a variety of environmental campaigns including efforts to save old timber stands from logging, to save pristine wilderness areas from mining operations, to protect the foothills east of the city and the National Forest near the ski basin from development, and to have the East Fork of the Jemez declared a National Recreation Area.

HOW TO USE THIS BOOK

The 45 hikes in this book are arranged according to geographical area. The map on page xx shows the approximate location of the hikes, and the chart on pages xxi-xxiii tells you the difficulty of a hike and the appropriate season.

The hikes are graded as "easy," "moderate," and "strenuous," but these terms are extremely loose and may mean different things to different hikers. It would probably be wise for a hiker new to the area to attempt one of the shorter hikes first to see how his or her rating compares with the editors'. In general we call a hike easy if it is under six miles in length and involves relatively little elevation change. A moderate hike is usually between six and ten miles, involves more uphill climbing and may be over less well maintained trails. A strenuous hike is over ten miles in length, usually involves substantial changes in elevation, is often at high elevations and sometimes is over very rough trails.

The term "cumulative uphill hiking" under ALTITUDE RANGE in each hike description is the estimated total number of feet you must walk uphill during that hike. Merely subtracting the lowest elevation point from the highest does not accurately describe a trail that involves a great deal of up and down hiking.

Weather conditions around Santa Fe vary widely from day to day and from season to season. If you have any doubt about the advisability of taking a hike, check with the Highway Department for road conditions and with the Santa Fe National Forest office for trail conditions.

Before you start on the hike, read through the preliminary material and the hiking directions to be sure that it's the kind of outing you have in mind. You might find from your reading that you'll want to take a camera or a wildflower field guide or binoculars for birding.

The sketch maps at the beginning of each chapter are not meant to be used as trail guides, but only to give a general idea of the length, direction and "shape" of the walk. We urge you to purchase the U.S. Geological Survey topographical map or other maps that cover the area of the hike in which you are interested. The topographical maps needed are listed at the beginning of each hike and are available at most sporting goods stores in Santa Fe or from the U.S. Geological Survey, Federal Center, Denver, CO 80225. If you're not familiar with these maps, spend some time studying them so that you'll recognize what the contour lines mean, which way is uphill or downhill, what the scale is and what the symbols mean. Compare it with the trail description and the sketch map in the book. It might be a good idea to pencil in on the topo map the route you'll be following. Even these maps occasionally contain errors and omissions. With experience, you'll probably learn to use not only the maps and the trail descriptions, but also your own intuition and outdoor skills to find your way in the wilderness.

In addition to the topo map, it will be helpful to have a New Mexico road map and also maps of the Santa Fe National Forest and the Carson National Forest where most of these hikes are located. These maps are available at the Santa Fe National Forest Office, Piñon Building, 1220 St. Francis Drive, Santa Fe, New Mexico. If you're hiking in the Sangre de Cristo Mountains, a map called "Pecos Wilderness" put out by the Santa Fe National Forest is helpful and is available at the address above.

You should take along a simple compass and a pencil and small memo pad. Usually the directions and turns on the trails are given as "left" or "right," but in several walks it is necessary to know the compass reading. The pencil and pad will be helpful so that you can make notes of starting times and odometer readings and can keep a record of how long it takes you to cover distances compared with the times given in the book.

Every effort has been made to make the directions, both driving and hiking, easy to understand and accurate. However, this book should not be considered a step-by-step, do-it-yourself hiking book for beginners. Because of changes in the routes of trails, vandalism of signs, destruction of landmarks, as well as the possibility of human error, accuracy of every detail cannot be guaranteed. Mileages given are necessarily inexact. If you haven't hiked in the mountains or remote areas before, don't start out alone with this guide as your only companion. Find a more experienced hiker to accompany you or join one of the Sierra Club outings which are scheduled every weekend and which are led by experienced hikers who are willing to share their knowledge with you. More information on these weekly hikes can be obtained by calling the Sierra Club office in Santa Fe.

One final word: wilderness is destructible, so when you are in it, respect it, love it and take care of it. Stay on the trails and don't take shortcuts. Pack out your trash to the last gum wrapper; even pack out somebody else's trash. Be careful with matches. Admire the flowers and rocks, but leave them there for the next passerby to admire, too. And remember that you are only visiting where other animals live, so treat them and their environment with the respect you'd like to receive where you live.

Happy hiking!

BACKGROUND OF SIERRA CLUB OUTINGS

by
Kenneth D. Adam

In 1892 a group of concerned and dedicated people met in San Francisco to form an organization, the Sierra Club, of those interested in mountain exploration. The first president was John Muir, and there were 182 charter members. The club's purposes included the publication of information about the mountains and enlisting the support and cooperation of the public and government in preserving the forests and natural features of the Sierra Nevada. It almost immediately took the lead in the successful battle to preserve Yosemite Valley and its high country as a National Park. The club held its first outing in 1901.

The Rio Grande Chapter came into being in 1963 with 52 members, and initially included not only New Mexico, but all of Texas and the eastern part of Arizona. Almost immediately most of Texas and all of Arizona formed their own chapters, leaving in the Rio Grande Chapter the state of New Mexico and the El Paso area of Texas. In the early 1970s the Santa Fe Group was formed, and soon had an active outings program.

Almost every week visitors to Santa Fe, as well as newly arrived and long-time residents, take advantage of the local Sierra Club hikes and ski trips, which are open to the public. This book is an attempt to satisfy the needs of those who like to hike on their own, but are frustrated by lack of information about how to reach a trailhead, or what to expect when they arrive there.

SAFETY TIPS FOR HIKERS

by
Herb Kincey, St. John's College Search and Rescue Team

Certain safety procedures should be followed by anyone going into wild country. Failure to observe these rules can lead to accidents or even death. Chances of becoming a statistic in the records of a search and rescue team will be greatly reduced by following these safety rules.

DO NOT GO ALONE: Unless you are experienced and prefer solitude, a party of at least four persons is recommended so that if one person is injured, one can remain with the victim while the other two go for help. Try never to leave an injured hiker alone.

PLAN YOUR ROUTE CAREFULLY: Know the escape routes. Plan a route ahead of time using U.S. Geological Survey and U.S. Forest Service maps. When traveling on foot allow about one hour for each two miles covered plus an additional hour for each 1000 feet of altitude gained. At all times know where you are on the map and the best way out to civilization.

GET WEATHER REPORTS AND BE PREPARED FOR EMER-GENCIES: Fast-moving frontal systems can bring sudden and violent changes in New Mexico weather, especially during winter. Try to obtain an extended weather forecast before setting out. Although even the highest peaks in New Mexico are considered "walkups" from a technical standpoint during summer months, nevertheless, they are above timberline and they are remote. On long hikes or scrambles above timberline the safe policy is to start for the summit at dawn and turn back about noon, the time when summer storms begin to form.

CHECK WITH AUTHORITIES: Most of the New Mexico high country lies within National Forests. Forest rangers know their districts and can offer valuable advice on trails, campsites and potential problems. Many desert lands are administered by the Bureau of Land Management (BLM), whose officials will be glad to help. The New Mexico Department of Game and Fish will make recommendations about where to hike during hunting seasons. A booklet from this department describes the areas open to hunters along with season dates. This is a useful publication for hikers wishing to avoid hunting areas. Bright clothing is appropriate for safety during big game hunting season.

GO PROPERLY EQUIPPED: As a rule the most serious dangers in the wilderness are WIND, COLD and WETNESS. Even during July it can snow on the higher peaks, and hard summer rains occur almost daily in the mountain range. It is quite possible to die from "exposure" (hypothermia) at any time of the year, especially above timberline (about 11,800 feet). Having warm clothing, even during the summer, is vital. A shirt, sweater, socks, mittens and cap (all of wool or polypropylene) should always be carried. Even when wet, wool is warm against the skin. For protection against wind and wetness carry a weatherproof parka or poncho. One of the first signs of hypothermia is shivering. This may be followed by difficulty walking and speaking, confusion, drowsiness and coma. Steps should be taken to restore and maintain body temperature as soon as signs of hypothermia appear. These steps may include locating shelter from the elements, use of warm clothing or blankets, replacing cold wet clothing, providing warm, non-alcoholic drinks and body-to-body transfer of heat. If symptoms intensify, medical help should be obtained as soon as possible.

Always carry these items with you when going into the back country: map, compass, flashlight, sunglasses, candle, waterproof matches, whistle, pocket knife, protective clothing, minimum first aid, extra food and water. Water is very scarce in some areas; carry plenty, at least a quart per person. Water purification tablets are recommended for water from streams or lakes. Giardia is now a common problem in wilderness areas.

ALLOW TIME FOR ACCLIMATIZATION: Persons going into high mountains from low altitudes should beware of trying to climb any of the major peaks until they have had a few days to acclimatize. Many people who go too high too fast suffer "mountain sickness." The symptoms are vomiting, diarrhea, and feeling very ill. Pulmonary edema, a major medical emergency, also can occur above the 8000-foot level. The symptoms include extreme fatigue or collapse, shortness of breath, a racking cough, bubbling noises in the chest, and bloody sputum. Unless transported to a much lower altitude immediately the victim may die within a matter of hours. If available, administer oxygen until reaching a hospital. Several other procedures may help prevent the "mountain miseries": arrive in good physical condition, get plenty of rest and sleep and avoid alcohol and smoking.

LEAVE INFORMATION WITH RELATIVES OR FRIENDS: An itinerary of your trip, along with the names and addresses of each member, description and license numbers of vehicles used, and expected time of return should be left with a reliable person. Once under way, stick to your planned route and schedule. Any time a group is seriously overdue or an accident has occurred, the New Mexico State Police should be called in order to obtain assistance.

LEARN THE LIMITATIONS OF EACH MEMBER: Assess the strengths and weaknesses of each member of the party. Do not try anything beyond the ability of the weakest hiker. Set the pace to that of the slowest hiker. Be willing to turn back when conditions warrant doing so.

KEEP THE PARTY TOGETHER: Individual members of a group should not be allowed to fall behind the main party or go ahead of it. Many wilderness fatalities have resulted from disregarding this rule. If the group is large, select one person to set the pace, another to bring up the rear. If hiking in the dark for some reason, assign each hiker a number and count off periodically.

WATCH FOR FLASH FLOODS: Most New Mexico streams are shallow and present few fording problems. However, flash floods occur in the steep arid canyons and arroyos around the perimeter of the mountains and in desert areas. Be especially careful in these hazardous areas and do not camp or leave vehicles parked there.

BEWARE OF LOOSE ROCK: In some places loose rock can be a serious hazard. Keep your group bunched together when going up or down this type of terrain. Never roll rocks down a mountainside. Another party may be below you.

GET OFF EXPOSED RIDGES DURING STORMS: Summer storms move in fast and will bring rain or hail, high winds, low visibility and lightning. Try not to allow your group to be caught on a peak or exposed ridge. If you are unable to get down in a lightning storm, have the group spread out with about 30 feet between each person. Stay away from lone trees or rocks. Avoid shallow caves or depressions, for ground currents may jump from the edge to your body. Insulate yourself from the ground (with pack, rope, clothing) and squat down, allowing only your feet to touch the ground or the improvised insulation. Do not lie down.

EMERGENCY SIGNALS: The following signals are considered standard by many search and rescue groups: Distress - 3 evenly spaced signals given within 30 seconds. Repeat as required. Acknowledgment - 2 signals given in quick succession. Return to Camp - 4 evenly spaced signals given within 30 seconds. Repeat as required.

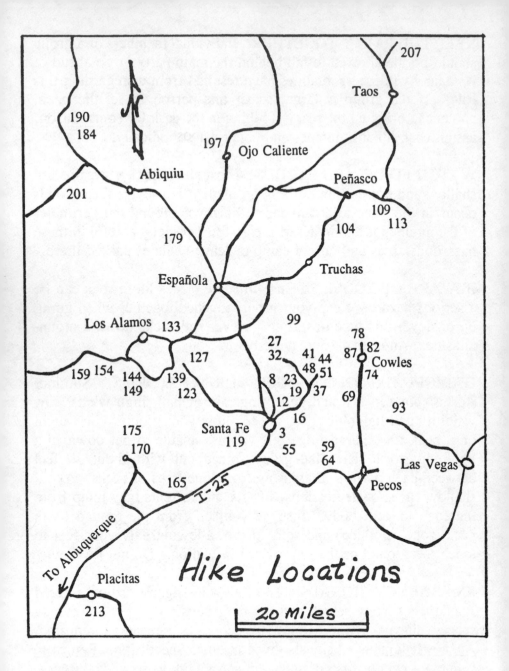

The numbers on the map above are the page numbers of the individual hike descriptions.

CHART OF HIKES

Difficulty: <u>E</u>=Easy, <u>M</u>=Moderate, <u>S</u>=Strenuous.

Season: Time of year when hike is most suitable is indicated by a bar.

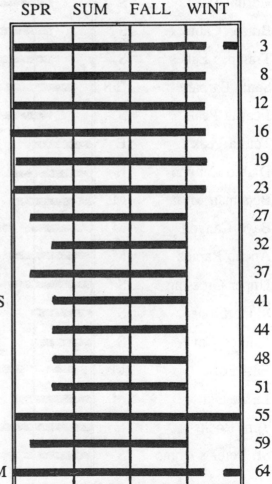

HIKE		SEASON				Page
		SPR	SUM	FALL	WINT	
Atalaya Mountain	M					3
Tesuque Creek	E					8
Chamisa Trail	E					12
Black Canyon	E					16
Hyde Park Circle	E					19
Borrego	M					23
Rancho Viejo	M					27
La Junta	S					32
Aspen Vista	E/S					37
Nambé Lake	M/S					41
La Vega	M					44
Santa Fe Baldy	S					48
Lake Katherine	S					51
Forest Road #79	E					55
Glorieta Baldy	S					59
Ghost Town	E/M					64

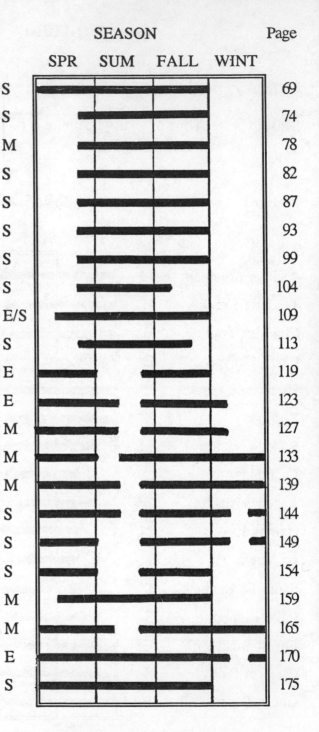

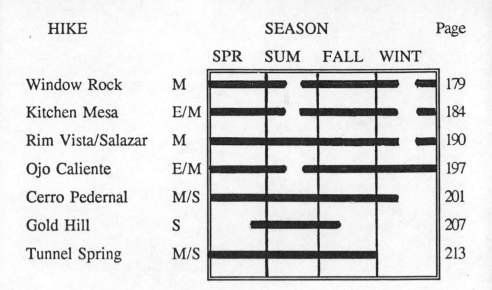

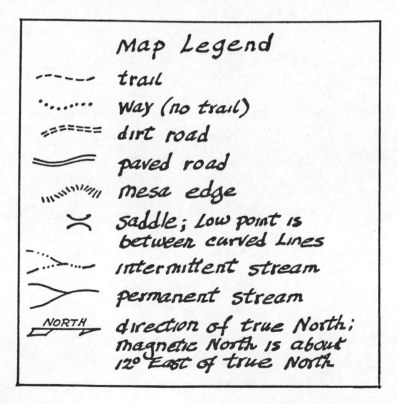

Map Legend

- – – – – trail
- ·········· way (no trail)
- ══════ dirt road
- ～～～ paved road
- ⅏ⅆⅉ mesa edge
- ⟩⟨ saddle; low point is between curved lines
- –·–·– intermittent stream
- ～～ permanent stream
- NORTH direction of true North; magnetic North is about 12° East of true North

DAY HIKES IN THE SANTA FE AREA

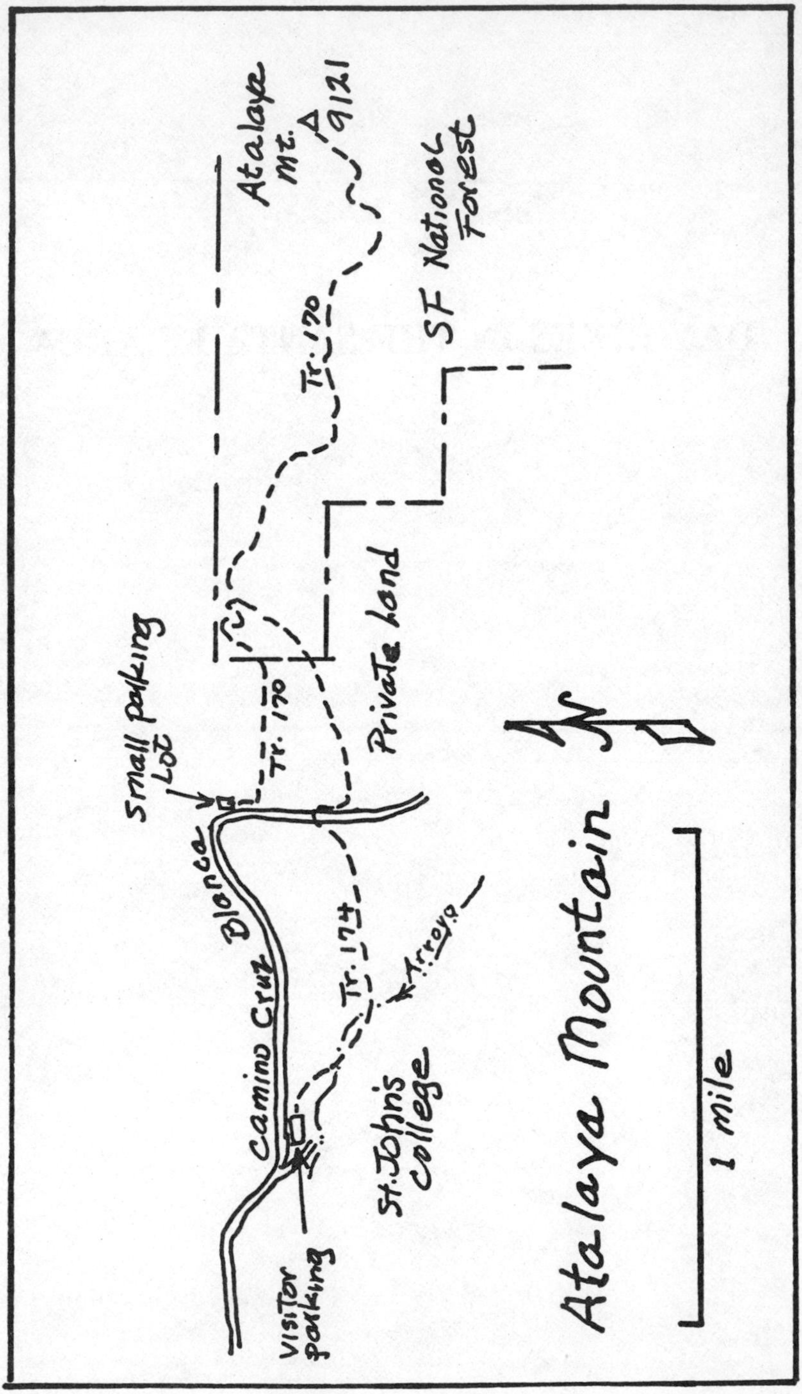

Atalaya Mountain

Atalaya Mt.
△ 9121

SF National Forest

Tr. 170

Private land

Small parking Lot

Camino Cruz Blanca

Tr. 170

Tr. 174

Arroyo

Visitor parking

St. John's College

1 mile

ATALAYA MOUNTAIN

by
Lionel Soracco

U.S. GEOLOGICAL SURVEY MAP REQUIRED: Santa Fe - 7.5 minute series.

SALIENT FEATURES: Atalaya (Spanish for "watchtower" or "height") is the ridge that rises just east of Santa Fe. This popular destination can be reached from two trailheads, one on Camino Cruz Blanca at the Ponderosa Ridge development, the other at St. John's College. The trail is mostly shaded and uphill through a forest which changes from piñon-juniper to ponderosa and Douglas fir and some white fir as you climb. At the top you'll have a full view of Santa Fe and the surrounding valley.

RATING: Moderate. This is a short but steep hike.

ROUND TRIP HIKING DISTANCE: Approximately 7 miles from the St. John's College Visitor's Parking Lot; approximately 5.5 miles from the Ponderosa Ridge parking area.

APPROXIMATE ROUND TRIP HIKING TIME: 3+ hours from Ponderosa Ridge, 4+ hours from St. John's College, stops not included.

ALTITUDE RANGE: Highest point, 9121 feet; lowest point, 7340 feet (St. John's) or 7540 feet (Ponderosa Ridge); cumulative uphill

3

hiking, 1781 feet (from St. John's) or 1581 feet (from Ponderosa Ridge).

SEASONAL CONSIDERATIONS: Can be hiked year round. It can be warm during the summer, so an early start is recommended. Carry at least a quart of water. During winter the trail is usually accessible, although there may be several inches of snow at the higher elevations and a foot or more at the top.

ROUND TRIP DRIVING: 5 miles to St. John's College, 6.5 miles to the Ponderosa Ridge/Camino Cruz Blanca trailhead; about 30 minutes.

DRIVING DIRECTIONS: From the northeast corner of the plaza, drive east (towards the mountains) on Palace Avenue one mile, crossing Paseo de Peralta and continuing to the intersection of Palace and Alameda. Turn left on Alameda. A few hundred yards past Smith Park, Alameda veers right (south) to become Camino Cabra. Continue south on Camino Cabra past Cristo Rey Church. About 0.7/mile past Cristo Rey, you'll pass the Los Miradores condominium development on your left. Turn left onto Camino Cruz Blanca at the St. John's College sign. If you're starting the hike at St. John's (Trail #174), turn right off Cruz Blanca into St. John's College, then immediately left into the Visitor's Parking Lot. The trailhead is at the far end of the lot.

If you're starting at the Ponderosa Ridge residential development (Trail #170), continue eastward on Camino Cruz Blanca 0.8/mile to where the road turns right (south). After turning, you'll be facing the entry gate to the Ponderosa Ridge-Wilderness Gate residential development. To your left is a small parking area with a large informational sign regarding Trail #170. Park here. Space is limited (a half-dozen cars at most).

4

HIKING INSTRUCTIONS: Trail #174 (St. John's trailhead) and Trail #170 (Ponderosa Ridge trailhead) intersect a short way up the mountain; from there to the top the trail is Trail #170.

First I'll describe Trail #174 to that intersection. Looking eastward from the parking lot, you'll see your destination, a long ridge rising gradually as it proceeds northwards. Starting at the far end of the parking lot, Trail #174 quickly winds down to the Arroyo de los Chamisos (dry except for a few weeks early in spring), crosses the arroyo, rises to traverse a field of chamisa bushes skirting St. John's new dormitory complex, recrosses the arroyo, and starts up a narrow creek bed. Signs will guide you.

After entering the small arroyo of the creek, you'll pass through a log maze built to discourage equestrians and cyclists. For the next quarter-mile, the trail follows the arroyo, with numerous "Stay on Trail" signs at creek crossings. A sign indicates where you leave the creek and head to the right and steeply upward to the Wilderness Gate Road.

Cross the road -- careful, there's occasional traffic here -- climb the steps and continue another quarter mile through woods to the log fence marking the entrance to the Santa Fe National Forest. Overhead are power lines running north-south across the foothills. A trail marker indicates that Atalaya is 2 miles distant. Climb up from the fence 40 yards, then turn left to follow Trail #174 another quarter mile to its intersection with Trail #170.

If you start the hike at the Ponderosa Ridge parking area (Trail #170), follow the wall south 50 yards to a gate. Turn left, through the gate, and continue uphill on the dirt road. You'll spot a house with a red metal roof. Just past that house the road veers right, but you continue straight ahead, passing under some powerlines and climbing wooden steps which lead to a log fence marking the Santa Fe National Forest boundary. Passing through the gate, follow the trail as it winds steeply uphill to its intersection with Trail #174.

<u>Note</u>: Both Trail #174 and Trail #170, from trailheads to log fences, pass through private property. Rights-of-way were negotiated over a period of years by the Sierra Club, Friends of Atalaya, Forest Trust, private landowners, and representatives of the Santa Fe National Forest. Respect this arrangement by keeping to the trails.

From the intersection to the top, you'll be on Trail #170. As this is a much-used trail, there are numerous "shortcuts" along the way. They are generally steeper and less secure than the main trail. We discourage their use.

The rest of Trail #170 is a well-worn shaded ascent through the forest. Notice the tree population gradually changing from piñon and juniper to ponderosa pine, Rocky Mountain juniper, and Douglas and white fir. Hiking in the summer, you'll experience gentle breezes and temperatures cooler than in the city below.

You'll reach the ridge a few hundred yards south of the summit. Turn left and follow the trail to the highest point, where you will be rewarded with a sweeping view of the city. Relax in the shade of the many trees and amuse yourself by identifying landmarks in Santa Fe. Can you spot your residence or hotel?

To return, reverse your course, but be careful: walking downhill, though easier, makes you potentially more prone to falls.

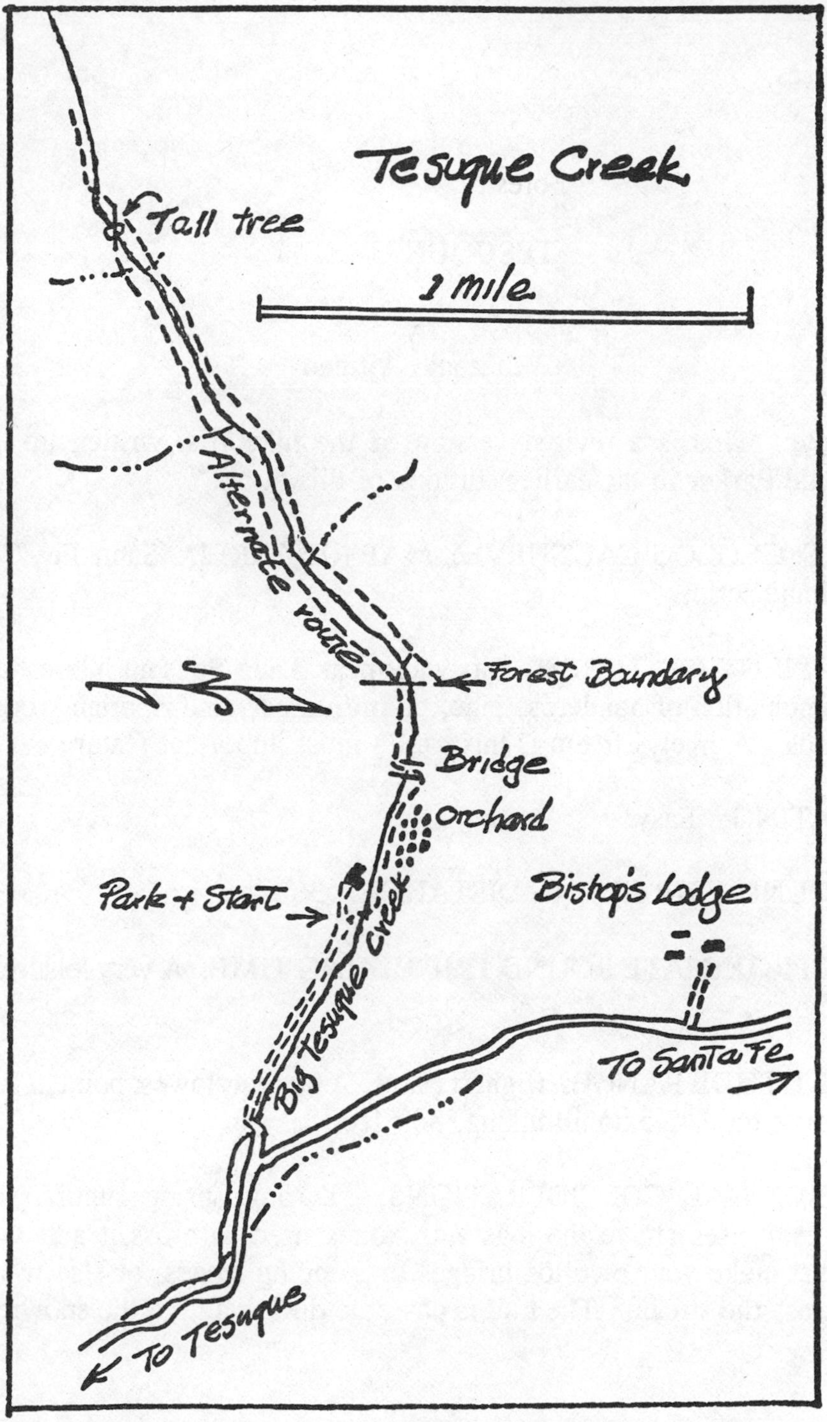

Tesuque Creek

Tall tree

1 mile

Alternate route

Forest Boundary

Bridge

Orchard

Park + Start

Bishop's Lodge

Big Tesuque Creek

To Santa Fe

To Tesuque

TESUQUE CREEK

by
Elizabeth Altman

<u>Note</u>: This is a revised version of the hike first written up by Katie Parker in the earlier editions of this book.

U.S. GEOLOGICAL SURVEY MAP REQUIRED: Santa Fe - 7.5 minute series.

SALIENT FEATURES: This walk near Santa Fe is an interesting combination of ponderosa pine, piñon/juniper, and riparian woodlands. A lively stream is this trail's most important feature.

RATING: Easy.

ROUND TRIP HIKING DISTANCE: 3 miles.

APPROXIMATE ROUND TRIP HIKING TIME: A very leisurely 2 hours.

ALTITUDE RANGE: Highest point, 7600 feet; lowest point, 7100 feet; cumulative uphill hiking, 500 feet.

SEASONAL CONSIDERATIONS: During spring runoff, the stream rises above the logs and stones used to cross it and you must make your own log bridges or stepping stones, or else wade across the stream. The trail is passable during all but the snowiest months. You should be prepared for snow on the south side of the stream during the winter months.

ROUND TRIP DRIVING: 8.2 miles; about half an hour.

DRIVING DIRECTIONS: From the plaza, drive north on Washington Avenue (which after about 4 blocks becomes Bishop's Lodge Road, Highway #590). In 3.5 miles, you will pass the entrance to Bishop's Lodge; almost exactly 1 mile beyond this entrance the paved road takes a 90-degree turn to the left, marked by a large yellow highway sign with an arrow pointing left. Don't take this left turn. Take instead the dirt road to the right, County Road #72A. Drive a short distance down this road until you come to a parking space in one of the two areas on the right identified as trail parking. The second sign says, "No Parking Beyond This Point." Respect the admonition, for if the parking privilege is abused by hikers then access to the trail along an easement over private land may be closed.

HIKING INSTRUCTIONS: Walk a short way up the road to a rock pillar and three 5-foot wooden posts. The trail begins immediately beyond the posts. Stay on the trail to avoid encroaching on private land. You will immediately cross Big Tesuque Creek on stepping stones. The trail follows the river upstream and passes an old abandoned vineyard and orchard on your right. After about 5 minutes you come out onto a dirt road. Note the sign on the left marking the trail back toward Tesuque that you just walked along. Go left over the car bridge and then turn right up the river. The trail follows the fence line. Look for woodpeckers in the cottonwood trees along the river bottom here.

In another 8 to 10 minutes, you will go through a Forest Service gate to enter the Santa Fe National Forest. There is a sign here giving the distances to Tesuque, Hyde State Park, and the Ski Basin. Be alert for bicyclists along this popular trail. Keep to the

9

right as the trail forks soon after the gate. (You will return on the left fork.) Trail #254 crosses the stream to the south side.

As you climb upward along a trail that parallels the creek, you will see signs of washes and trails leading off from the main trail. Keep to the main trail that leads upward to a rubble-covered hill where the trail splits. Take the left fork, where a sign will confirm that you are on the Winsor Trail. Continue along as the trail rises 20-50 feet above the creek.

About thirty minutes into the hike, you will come to another stream crossing; you have just passed the return trail. Go back about 30 yards from the stream and you will notice a trail heading down toward the river past a huge ponderosa pine. This is your return trail and involves another stream crossing. You may wish to return at this point and cross to the north side of the creek to make a walk of about 3 miles. Or, you may continue past the return trail to a creek crossing and then as far up the trail as you wish. If you do continue the hike, you will cross the creek several times.

When you return, look for the trail by the large ponderosa pine that crosses the creek to the north side where the vegetation, soil, and temperature are markedly different from the south side. Stop occasionally to look back up the canyon; at one point you will be able to see the radio towers above the Ski Basin. When you reach the large wooden bridge, cross the bridge and turn right onto the trail that you came in on that goes alongside the old orchard. The road straight ahead goes past a metal gate and leads to Bishop's Lodge and other private property.

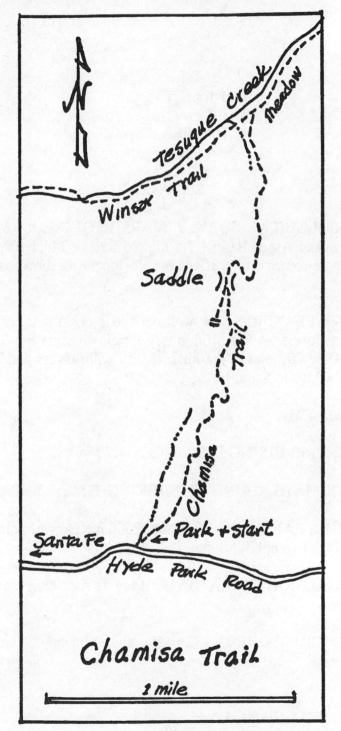

Chamisa Trail

1 mile

CHAMISA TRAIL

by
Bill Stone

U.S. GEOLOGICAL SURVEY MAPS REQUIRED: McClure Reservoir and Aspen Basin - 7.5 minute series. Much of the trail has been re-routed and portions are no longer as shown on these maps.

SALIENT FEATURES: A well-defined mountain trail through evergreen forest. A beautiful grassy meadow beside Big Tesuque Creek at the far point of the hike. Many wildflowers and birds in season. Close to Santa Fe.

RATING: Easy.

ROUND TRIP HIKING DISTANCE: 4.75 miles.

APPROXIMATE ROUND TRIP HIKING TIME: 2½-3 hours.

ALTITUDE RANGE: Highest point, 8500 feet; lowest point, 7800 feet; cumulative uphill hiking, 1240 feet.

SEASONAL CONSIDERATIONS: May be snowed-in and icy in midwinter.

ROUND TRIP DRIVING: 12 miles; approximately 30 minutes.

DRIVING DIRECTIONS: From the plaza, drive north on Washington Avenue 6 blocks and turn right on Artist Road. There is a sign here pointing to Hyde State Park and the Ski Basin. Measure your mileage from the turn. Drive 5.6 miles to where there is a wide canyon on the north (left) side of the road. Park in the off-road parking spaces on either side of the road. The trail starts uphill near the road on the north side. There is a US Forest Service sign saying "Trail 183 - Big Tesuque 2¼." This is the Chamisa Trail.

HIKING INSTRUCTIONS: The trail goes due east for a few hundred feet and climbs sharply. It then turns due north. It is deeply forested, with piñon, two species of juniper, and ponderosa pine at the start. There are many switchbacks, and as you climb higher there are views of the canyon and Hyde Park Road. Gambel oak and Douglas fir now appear. White (limber) pine and white fir appear at higher elevations. The trail is narrow, and at some places proceeds along a steep dugway, with little room to pass another person. The footing here is loose and sandy.

After you have walked a mile and a quarter and climbed 700 feet, you will come to the crest of the trail (altitude 8500 feet). A trail coming up the canyon from the left meets Trail #183 here. This is a good place for a break.

The trail now goes downhill. It turns sharply southeast, to your right as you approach, then, after a few hundred feet, toward the northeast (left), and continues in a northerly direction for the rest of the hike. It proceeds down a dry stream bed (very wet in spring). The footing is rocky in places. Aspen is found here as well as the trees mentioned above.

After one mile you come to a small grassy meadow. Continue about a quarter of a mile and you will see two posts driven into the ground. This is the junction with the Winsor Trail (#254). The Chamisa Trail ends here. There is a grassy meadow northeast (upstream) of the junction, and the Big Tesuque Creek is on its western border. The meadow is a beautiful, quiet spot and a good place to have your lunch. There is a large granite boulder in the middle of the meadow. The altitude is 7960 feet. This is the furthest point of the hike.

Return the way you came. Be sure to get back on the same trail (Chamisa), by turning left (south) at the two posts. The Chamisa Trail is level at this point. (The Winsor Trail follows the Big Tesuque downstream.) The 540-foot climb back to the saddle is moderate in most places, but very steep in two. On reaching the saddle again (8500 feet) the trail divides. The trail to the left, which is level here, is the trail you came up on. The other trail goes steeply down into the canyon and will eventually return you to the parking area. Proceed to the trailhead.

Many wildflowers and plants may be seen along this trail. Among the predominant ones are Oregon grape, yucca, scarlet gilia, red penstemon, lupine (slopes near the crest are covered with its blooms in the late spring), and many Compositae. In addition, you may see mullein, yellow evening primrose, yarrow, wild iris, salsify, and coneflower in the meadows.

I have seen 42 species of birds along the Chamisa Trail. Among them are hawks, hummingbirds, woodpeckers, flycatchers, swallows, jays, ravens, nuthatches, chickadees, thrushes, warblers, vireos, and the sparrow types.

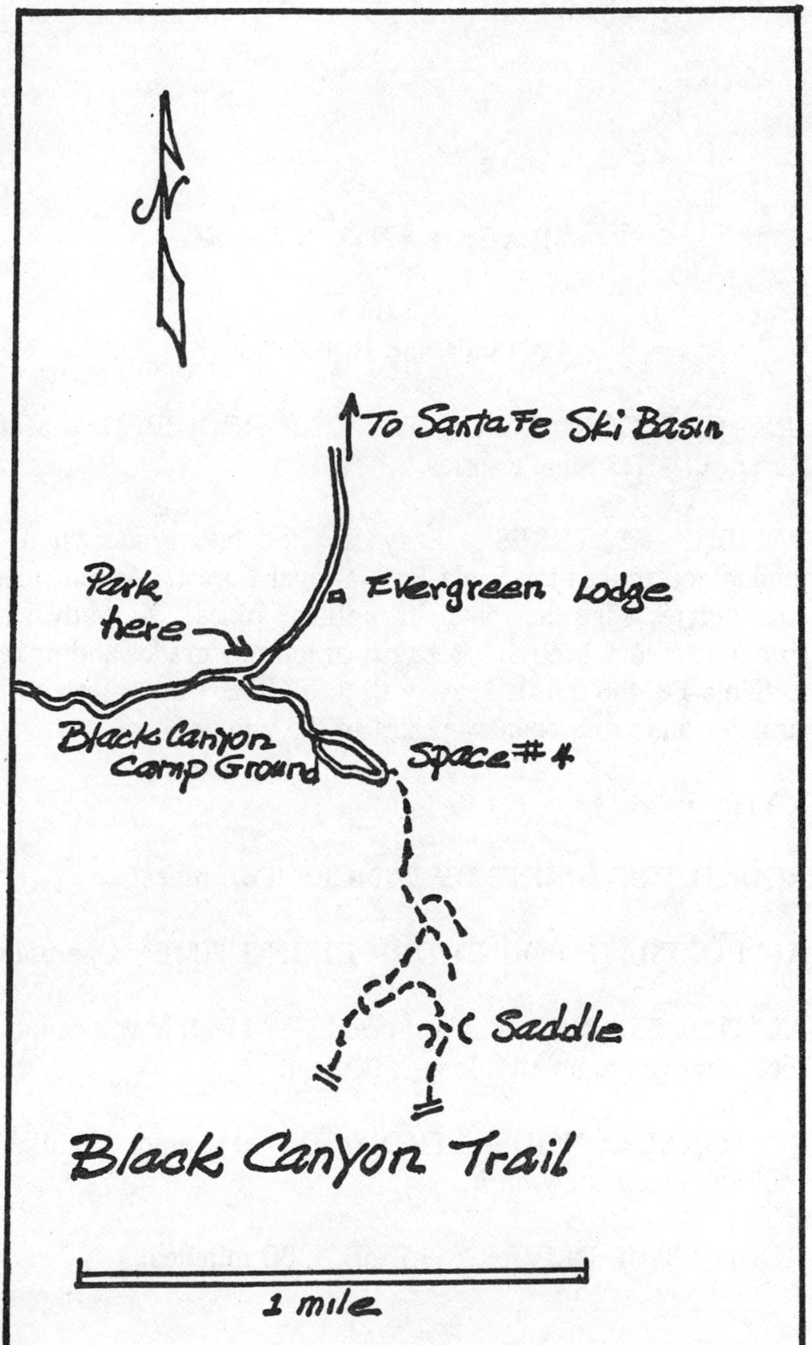

N

To Santa Fe Ski Basin

Park here →

Evergreen Lodge

Black Canyon Camp Ground

Space #4

Saddle

Black Canyon Trail

1 mile

WH

BLACK CANYON TRAIL

by
Linda and Bill Zwick

U.S. GEOLOGICAL SURVEY MAP REQUIRED: McClure Reservoir - 7.5 minute series.

SALIENT FEATURES: Easy to moderate grade on a well-maintained trail in the Santa Fe National Forest. Aspen trees and strawberries edge the route through the pines. A shady walk in summer, colorful in fall. Because of its easy grades and proximity to Santa Fe, the trail is heavily used by hikers and campers in the summer and cross country skiers in the winter.

RATING: Easy.

ROUND TRIP HIKING DISTANCE: Two miles.

APPROXIMATE ROUND TRIP HIKING TIME: One hour.

ALTITUDE RANGE: Highest point, 8800 feet; lowest point, 8300 feet; cumulative uphill hiking, 500 feet.

SEASONAL CONSIDERATIONS: Do not attempt this hike when trail has much snow on it.

ROUND TRIP DRIVING: 15 miles; 30 minutes.

DRIVING DIRECTIONS: From the plaza, drive north on Washington Avenue 6 blocks and turn right on Artist Road. There is a sign here pointing to Hyde State Park and the Ski Basin. Measure your mileage from the turn. Drive 7 miles to the Black Canyon Campground and park on your right outside the campground entrance along the rail fence as indicated by the parking signs. There is no fee for cars parked outside the fence.

HIKING INSTRUCTIONS: Begin your walk by following the paved road through Black Canyon Campground, being considerate of the paying campers by keeping your dog leashed and by staying on the road. Follow the road uphill until you reach Space 4 in a group of campsites at the highest point of the campground. Just beyond Space 4 is the trail sign where the graveled trail begins.

Approximately one-half mile from the beginning of the trail, the trail forks. At this point, there is a sign with a double-headed arrow indicating the trail goes either way. Take the left fork for a few yards to where you see a rocky wash straight ahead. Do not go up the wash; rather, look for the trail switching back to the left. Follow the trail up to where it crosses the wash close to the saddle of the ridge. Continue along this trail to the saddle where you will see "No Trespassing" signs on the trails leading into protected watershed land. After taking a break at the top, you will see a well-worn, wider trail to the west. It has beautiful views toward the Jemez Mountains. Use this trail to return to where the trail forked, then go back the way you came up from Space 4.

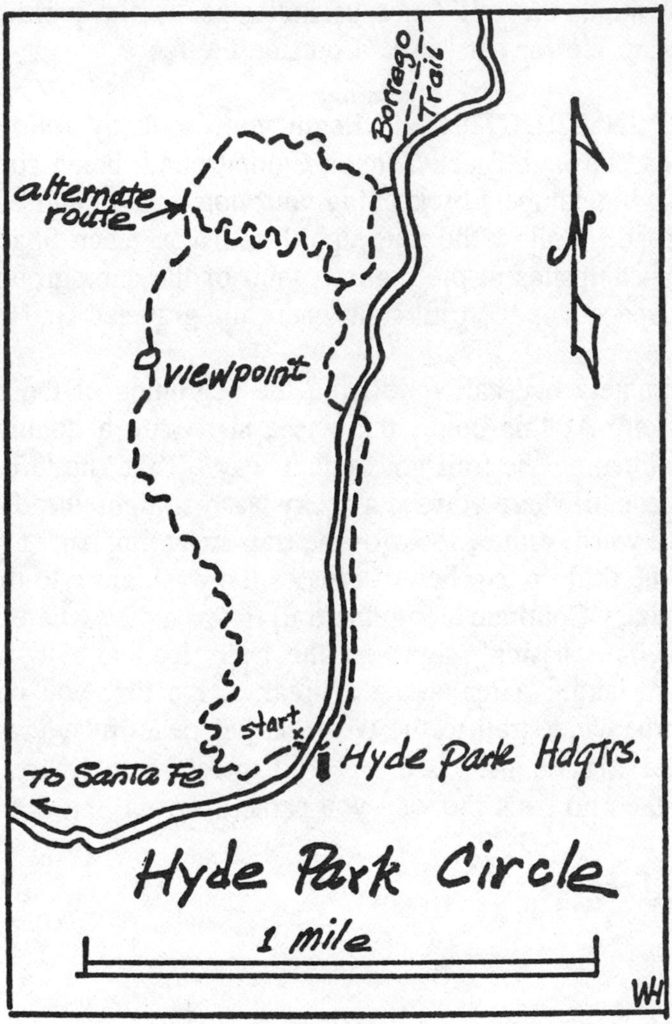

Borrego Trail

N

alternate route

viewpoint

start

To Santa Fe

Hyde Park Hdqtrs.

Hyde Park Circle

1 mile

WH

HYDE MEMORIAL PARK CIRCLE

by
John H. Muchmore

U.S. GEOLOGICAL SURVEY MAP REQUIRED: McClure Reservoir - 7.5 minute series (the trail described below is not shown on the map).

SALIENT FEATURES: Short drive from Santa Fe over paved road. Well-marked (with blazes) and maintained trail; includes Girl Scout nature trail. Site of early Santa Fe logging activity. Stands of piñon, ponderosa, spruce, fir, Gambel oak and wildflowers. Excellent 360-degree view of Lake and Tesuque Peaks, the ski basin and the Sandia and Jemez Mountains. The real value of this walk will be obtained by strolling and stopping frequently.

RATING: Easy, but with steep trails.

ROUND TRIP HIKING DISTANCE: 5 miles.

APPROXIMATE ROUND TRIP HIKING TIME: 3 hours.

ALTITUDE RANGE: Highest point, 9400 feet; lowest point, 8400 feet; cumulative uphill hiking, 1000 feet.

SEASONAL CONSIDERATIONS: Good four season walk, unless heavily snowed in.

ROUND TRIP DRIVING: 16 miles; approximately 45 minutes.

DRIVING DIRECTIONS: From the plaza, drive north on Washington Avenue 6 blocks and turn right on Artist Road. There is a sign here pointing to Hyde State Park and the Ski Basin. Measure your mileage from the turn. Drive 7.4 miles to Hyde Memorial State Park Headquarters on your right. There are parking spaces in a large lot below the headquarters on the right-hand side of the road and in a smaller lot above the headquarters on the left side. Pay your entrance and use fees at the self-service payment box. The trailhead is directly across the road from the stone store and is marked by a "Hiking Trail" sign.

HIKING INSTRUCTIONS: Begin your walk by crossing Little Tesuque Creek on the stone bridge opposite the general store, then by turning left (south). The trail, well marked with tree blazes, climbs steeply through a series of switchbacks, then gradually levels off as it serpentines along an ascending ridge. Check your watch as you cross the bridge, and plan to stop at half hour intervals to view the surrounding vistas and enjoy the distant mountains. At your first stop, you will be about 500 feet above the campground. Looking ahead to the northeast, you will see the Santa Fe Ski Basin with the watershed rising to Tesuque and Lake Peaks. Behind you to the southeast, Thompson Peak is showing above the Black Canyon notch. At your next stop, northwest and southwest views should have your attention. Southwesterly are the Sandia and Ortiz Mountains. Westerly and northwesterly are the Jemez Peaks with the Buckman flats and the Caja del Rio in the middle foreground.

Your trail now rollercoasts along the ridge and another five minutes brings you to a 360-degree view point. There are two picnic tables here that invite you to stop for lunch or a snack. Although downed timber gives evidence of some harsh winter weather, this trail's southern ascent makes it inviting even during years of heavy snows. Turn-of-the-century logging is evident along the ridge. A word of caution: during summer thunderstorm activity, portions of this ridge have taken direct lightning strikes --

you will see several large trees that have been hit by lightning.

As you continue along the ridge, you will see a branch of the trail just beyond the first picnic table. This right-branching trail will bring you down a series of switchbacks to the recreational vehicle hookup section of the Hyde Park Campground and will cut off about 30 minutes of your walking circuit. However, we suggest that you continue straight ahead past the second picnic table. The main trail continues a gradual traversing descent along the northeast or right side of the main ridge.

Within five minutes, your trail swings sharply to the east (your right) and drops steeply through a series of descending switchbacks to the trail's end at the northern boundary of the Hyde Park Campground. As you leave the trail, the paved Ski Basin road will be directly in front of you and can be followed down to your car. However, let us avoid the paved road. There are a series of short trails running down the canyon approximately 50 to 100 feet above the west side of the road. Keeping the paved road on your left, follow any of these interesting trails until you pass the recreational vehicle section. You will soon cross the alternate descending trail from the ridge above you. This trail almost immediately converges with the Girl Scout nature trail with its metal and wooden identification signs pointing out various types of trees, shrubs and wildflowers. The nature trail continues for about ten minutes and soon returns you to the paved road. At this point, cross the paved road, then Little Tesuque Creek, and then follow any of the dirt roads or trails that follow the creek back down to the Park Headquarters, the store and your car.

The entire circuit can be covered in three leisurely hours. With a picnic and a clear warm day the circuit could be extended to all day. Snow cover may require three strenuous hours for the circuit. Experienced hikers will walk this trail in under two hours. Novices should not attempt it in deep snow.

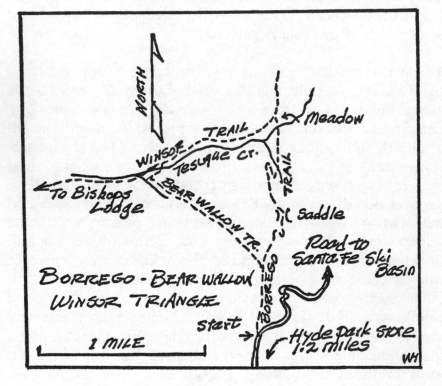

NORTH

WINSOR TRAIL

Meadow

TESUQUE CT.

BEAR WALLOW TR.

BORREGO

TRAIL

To Bishops Lodge

Saddle

Road to Santa Fe Ski Basin

BORREGO - BEAR WALLOW WINSOR TRIANGLE

Start

Hyde Park Store 1.2 miles

1 MILE

WH

22

BORREGO-BEAR WALLOW-WINSOR TRIANGLE

by
Bill Chudd

U.S. GEOLOGICAL SURVEY MAPS REQUIRED: Aspen Basin, and, for the first five or six hundred yards only, McClure Reservoir - 7.5 minute series.

SALIENT FEATURES: An easily accessible short hike along good trails, partly stream-side, and through pleasant woods rife with seasonal wildflowers. You will make two stream crossings. If spring runoff is unusually high, the crossings can present some problems.

RATING: Easy.

ROUND TRIP HIKING DISTANCE: 4 miles.

APPROXIMATE ROUND TRIP HIKING TIME: 2 hours 15 minutes, with stops.

ALTITUDE RANGE: Highest point, 8880 feet; lowest point, 8240 feet; cumulative uphill hiking, 760 feet.

SEASONAL CONSIDERATIONS: Usually snowed-in in midwinter. Can be hot in midsummer, but is fairly well shaded.

ROUND TRIP DRIVING: 17.5 miles; approximately 40 minutes.

DIVING DIRECTIONS: From the plaza, drive north on Washington Avenue 6 blocks and turn right on Artist Road. There is a sign here pointing to Hyde State Park and the Ski Basin. Measure your mileage from the turn. Drive a little over 8.5 miles to the small paved parking area on the left side of the road. To alert you to your approach, you will notice an RV parking area at the left of the road 0.2/mile before the Borrego Trail parking area.

HIKING INSTRUCTIONS: The trail starts down from the far left corner of the parking lot. There is a sign identifying this as the Borrego Trail #150 and giving the distance to Big Tesuque Creek as one and a half miles. After 4 or 5 twists, the trail becomes wide and easy to follow. You have entered a lovely forest of firs, aspens and, shortly, a few ponderosa pines. Later you may see some shrubby Gambel oaks trying valiantly to become full-fledged trees.

This is the Borrego Trail along which shepherds brought their flocks to market in Santa Fe from towns to the north, before modern roads and other developments made life easier and less interesting. In about half a mile the trail passes between two wooden signposts. If these remain intact, the left hand one will point out the Bear Wallow Trail, with Big Tesuque Creek 1 mile away. The right hand sign will show the Borrego Trail, #150, with Big Tesuque Creek and the Winsor Trail #254, 1¼ miles ahead. Take the left fork, the Bear Wallow Trail, #182, which heads west of north. (You will return on the right fork.) After about 15 minutes you will get glimpses through the trees ahead of a transverse ridge, indicating your approach to Big Tesuque Creek. Begin listening for the always pleasant sound of its flow. Continue down the switchbacks to the stream bank, one mile from the Borrego Trail.

There is usually a somewhat flimsy log crossing a bit downstream from the trail. Cross the creek at the trail or over the log bridge. The Winsor Trail #254, marked by a sign, parallels the stream.

Your route will be upstream, a right turn after crossing the creek. If the season is right, look around for raspberries in this vicinity. Other berries you are apt to encounter in the course of this hike are strawberries (many plants but few berries); edible (but not choice) thimbleberries; non-poisonous (but hardly edible unless cooked or prepared) Oregon grape and kinnikinnick; and poisonous baneberry.

Make the right turn and continue on the Winsor trail. It's all upstream and uphill, but you knew you'd have to pay for all that lovely downhill trail behind you. Note the ridge on your right, across the creek. Eventually, you're going to have to get over that. After one mile, you will reach the junction of the Winsor and the Borrego trails. Turn right, southeast, through a small meadow, onto the Borrego Trail. You will shortly cross the Big Tesuque Creek. A huge fallen ponderosa over the creek will make your crossing easier. Soon thereafter attack the ridge you saw earlier by a winding switchback trail. After topping the ridge, the trail descends for a while, levels off, and then returns to the junction with Bear Wallow Trail which comes in from the right. You have now completed a triangle of the Bear Wallow, Winsor and Borrego Trails, each leg about one mile.

Continue up the Borrego Trail one-half mile to your car. Next time, take this circuit in the reverse direction. It will seem like a different walk.

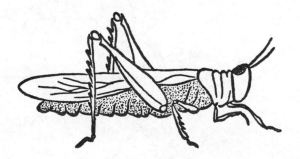

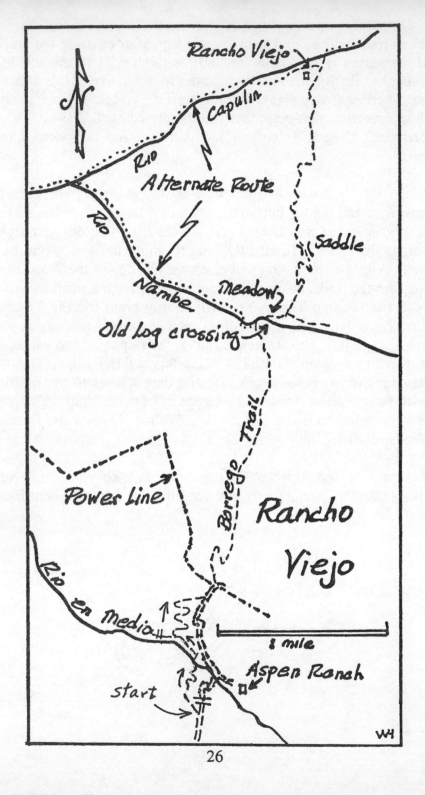

RANCHO VIEJO

by
Betsy Fuller

U.S. GEOLOGICAL SURVEY MAP REQUIRED: Aspen Basin - 7.5 minute series.

SALIENT FEATURES: Lovely meadows and fast-running clear streams; wildflowers in season and good stands of ponderosa, spruce, fir, aspen. Not recommended for low-slung cars. During winter, the road from the Ski Basin down to the "T" junction of #102 and #412 is closed to vehicular traffic and reserved for skiers.

Note: The beginning and end of this hike are on new trails constructed in the fall of 1994 by the US Forest Service in order to avoid trespassing on Indian land. Some of these instructions may seem overly detailed, since by the time you take this hike the Forest Service may have put in signs at the various junctions. In any case, do not go through the gates and fences onto Indian land.

RATING: Moderate/strenuous.

ROUND TRIP HIKING DISTANCE: 11.5 miles.

APPROXIMATE ROUND TRIP HIKING TIME: 6½ hours.

ALTITUDE RANGE: Highest point, 9200 feet; lowest point, 8187 feet; cumulative uphill hiking, 2300 feet.

SEASONAL CONSIDERATIONS: Not a winter hike.

ROUND TRIP DRIVING: 34 miles; approximately 2 hours.

DRIVING DIRECTIONS: From the plaza, drive north on Washington Avenue 6 blocks and turn right on Artist Road. There is a sign here pointing to Hyde State Park and the Ski Basin. Measure your mileage from the turn. At about 12 miles (0.5/mile beyond the Big Tesuque picnic area) turn left onto the Pacheco Canyon Road (Forest Road #102) and continue for 3 miles until the road comes to a "T" junction with Forest Road #412. Take your mileage here again. Turn right on Forest Road #412 and continue on up over the ridge (on a sometimes very bumpy road), passing several secondary roads and an old corral up the hill to your right. About 1.3 miles beyond the junction of #412 and #102, you will come to a flat parking area on the right side of the road. Park here.

HIKING INSTRUCTIONS: Walk about 100 yards farther along the road to the trailhead on the left side of the road. The trail starts uphill and winds through a mixed forest of pines and occasional aspens. Then it descends via switchbacks to the Rio en Medio, a small, easily-crossed stream (possibly more impressive during spring runoff).

Cross the stream and go up the opposite bank until you come to the old Rio en Medio Trail (about 20-25 feet from the crossing). Although you turn to the left here, take a look up the trail to the right and you will see a fence and a gate. On the return trip, these will help you mark the place where your trail -- the one you've just come up on -- takes off to cross the creek.

Turn left and walk downstream on the old Rio en Medio Trail for several hundred feet until you see a trail branching off to the right, uphill. Follow this trail as it zigzags up the hill until it joins the old Lucky Star Mine road. Turn left here (noting this junction for your return). Follow the road uphill until you come to a saddle where the road turns sharply to the right. Leave the road here and look for a trail that starts downhill to the north. The Forest Service unimaginatively calls this Trail #150, but it is part of the historic Borrego Trail which as recently as the mid-20th century was used to herd sheep from the high mountains east of Chimayo and Truchas to Santa Fe. As you walk down the small drainage, you'll be going through a dark forest of spruce and fir. In the summer, you may see the spectacular flowering green gentian, which sometimes grows as tall as 5 feet, and, if there is any water in the small drainage, watch for the one-sided pyrola in the wet dirt.

After about a mile and a half of steady descent, you'll first hear and then arrive at the Rio Nambé which flows toward the west on down to the Nambé Indian Pueblo about 6 miles downstream. Cross the river to the north bank. For many years there has been a huge fallen ponderosa pine lying across the river from bank to bank. However, this log has disintegrated to such an extent that, by the time this book is published, it will surely be impassable for anyone bigger than a chipmunk. Instead, you will have to cross the river by wading across (and having wet feet the rest of the trip) or by scouting up and down the river for stepping stones or another fallen log.

Just upstream from the crossing, you will find yourself in a lovely open meadow. This is a good spot for your first rest stop and snack, especially since the next mile and a half will involve climbing from an elevation of about 8200 to 8800 feet. After your rest, continue on upstream for about a quarter of a mile. At this point you will see the trail divide, one branch going on up the river and the other (still your Trail #150) going to the left (north) up the slope away from the river. You will be climbing through ponderosa pines, and the trail is lined with mountain mahogany which you can identify by its curlicue seeds. As you top the ridge and start down the trail on the north-facing slope into the Rio Capulin (chokecherry) valley, you'll be going through aspen forests and an occasional scrub oak grove.

It's approximately 2.5 miles from the Rio Nambé crossing where you had your snack to the Rio Capulin. Walk downstream for a few hundred yards and you will find the burned-out remains of a log cabin that was once used by the sheepherders of the old Spanish ranch known as Rancho Viejo. Have a good rest in this lovely sloping meadow because retracing your steps back to your car will be more strenuous than the outbound trip, especially the long last ascent out of the Rio Nambé valley.

Return the way you came. If you come to a gate as you are walking down the old Lucky Star Mine road, then you have missed the place where your trail takes off to zigzag down to the Rio en Medio. Walk back up the road about 75 yards and you will see the trail you came up on. Also, if you come to the gate on the Rio en Medio Trail, turn back for about 50 yards and you will see where the trail heads down the bank to the stream crossing.

Someday, you may want to extend this walk by going downstream from the burned-out cabin along the Rio Capulin to the junction of this stream with the Rio Nambé and then back up the Nambé to the fallen log near which you crossed several hours before. This added loop would increase your hike by about 3 miles.

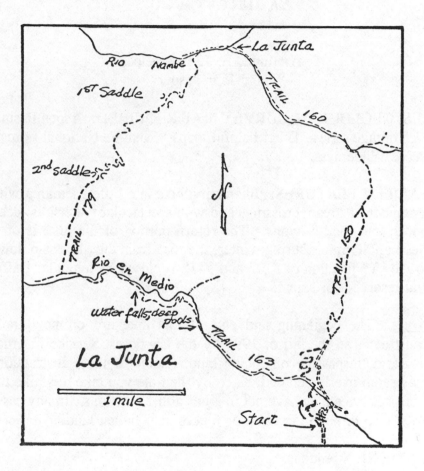

Rio Nambe

La Junta

1st Saddle

TRAIL 160

2nd saddle

TRAIL 179

Rio en Medio

TRAIL 150

water falls, deep pools

TRAIL 163

La Junta

1 mile

Start

LA JUNTA CIRCUIT

by
Art Judd, E. J. Evangelos,
and John Jasper

U.S. GEOLOGICAL SURVEY MAP REQUIRED: Aspen Basin - 7.5 minute series. Other helpful maps: Santa Fe National Forest, Pecos Wilderness.

SALIENT FEATURES: Interesting hike in a little-used area with a number of stream crossings and with spectacular waterfalls, deep pools, and rock canyons. The return portion of the hike is on a steep uphill trail. During winter, the road from the Ski Basin down to the "T" junction of #102 and #412 is closed to vehicular traffic and reserved for skiers.

Note: The beginning and end of this hike are on new trails constructed in the fall of 1994 by the US Forest Service in order to avoid trespassing on Indian land. Some of these instructions may seem overly detailed, since by the time you take this hike the Forest Service may have put in signs at the junctions. In any case, do not go through the gates or fences onto Indian land.

RATING: Strenuous.

ROUND TRIP HIKING DISTANCE: About 13 miles, but the hike feels longer due to elevation changes.

APPROXIMATE ROUND TRIP HIKING TIME: About 7½ hours, not including rest, meal and photo opportunity stops.

ALTITUDE RANGE: Highest point, 9200 feet; lowest point, 7640 feet; cumulative uphill hiking, 2800 feet.

SEASONAL CONSIDERATIONS: Usually open May 1st to October 1st. This will vary depending upon snow conditions. River crossing could be difficult during the early spring runoff.

ROUND TRIP DRIVING: Approximately 34 miles; 2 hours.

DRIVING DIRECTIONS: From the plaza, drive north on Washington Avenue 6 blocks and turn right on Artist Road. There is a sign here pointing to Hyde State Park and the Ski Basin. Measure your mileage from the turn. At about 12 miles (0.5/mile beyond the Big Tesuque picnic area) turn left onto the Pacheco Canyon Road (Forest Road #102) and continue for 3 miles until the road comes to a "T" junction with Forest Road #412. Take your mileage here again. Turn right on Forest Road #412 and continue on up over the ridge (on a sometimes very bumpy road), passing several secondary roads and an old corral up the hill to your right. About 1.3 miles beyond the junction of #412 and #102, you will come to a flat parking area on the right side of the road. Park here.

HIKING INSTRUCTIONS: Walk about 100 yards farther along the road to the trailhead on the left side of the road. The trail starts uphill and winds through a mixed forest of pines and occasional aspens. Then it descends via switchbacks to the Rio en Medio, a small, easily-crossed stream (possibly more impressive during spring runoff).

Cross the stream and go up the opposite bank until you come to the old Rio en Medio Trail (about 20-25 feet from the crossing). Although you turn to the left here, take a look up the trail to the right and you will see a fence and a gate. On the return trip, these will help you mark the place where your trail -- the one you've just come up on -- takes off to cross the creek.

Turn left and walk downstream on the old Rio en Medio Trail for several hundred feet until you see a trail branching off to the right, uphill. Follow this trail as it zigzags up the hill until it joins the old Lucky Star Mine road. Turn left here. Follow the road uphill until you come to a saddle where the road turns sharply to the right. Leave the road here and look for a trail that starts downhill to the north.

The trail makes a steep descent for about 1.7 miles to the Rio Nambé. The Rio Nambé begins to make itself heard as you near the last quarter mile or so. Just before you get to the river, notice the huge moss-covered boulder on the left of the trail. In the spring, garlands of wildflowers bedeck this rock.

At the Rio Nambé, take Trail #160 downstream for a few hundred yards and either ford the river or cross on dead-fall. Continue on down the river for about half an hour (a little over a mile) to the junction of the Rio Nambé with the Rio Capulin (La Junta means the meeting point). You'll come to a fork in the trail when you get close to this junction. Take either one; they both lead to La Junta. The Rio Capulin comes in from the right. Cross it and continue on downstream for several hundred yards to the junction of your trail (#160) with Trail #179. A sign marking this junction is tacked onto a large ponderosa pine, so watch for it. Trail #179 crosses the river here. Usually adequate dead-fall bridges the river at this point. Cross with care, especially in early spring and on frosty mornings, as the tree trunks are often coated with ice and can be very slippery.

After crossing the river, Trail #179 climbs up a deeply scoured arroyo. After about 45 minutes on this trail, you'll top out at a saddle -- a good place for a rest and a snack. The trail now turns downhill, passes through another valley and then ascends to the top of another saddle. At one place on this portion of the hike, the trail divides -- take the left trail which switches back and forth to the second saddle. The power line crosses the trail here and you will now begin the one-mile descent to the Rio en Medio, a total of three miles from La Junta. Just before reaching the Rio en Medio, a trail sign states "Aspen Meadow 3 miles." A sharp left turn here onto Trail #163 will take you up the Rio en Medio, the first stream you crossed at the beginning of the hike. At the junction, Trail #163 may be narrow and heavy with vegetation.

This is probably the most beautiful and strenuous leg of this lovely hike: three miles of waterfalls, deep pools, rock canyons, wild-flowers, mushrooms, and trout. The trail crosses the Rio en Medio numerous times and goes steeply up to gain the elevation lost in the descent to La Junta. It's about 3.5 steep miles up the Rio en Medio to the place where you will cross back over the stream to return to your car. If you come to the fence across the trail, you've gone too far. Walk back about 50 yards from the fence and you will see where the trail goes down the bank to cross the stream.

To return to Santa Fe, either go back up the Pacheco Canyon Road the way you came or continue down Forest Road #412 past Vigil Meadows on the left to Rancho Encantado and the village of Tesuque and back to Santa Fe.

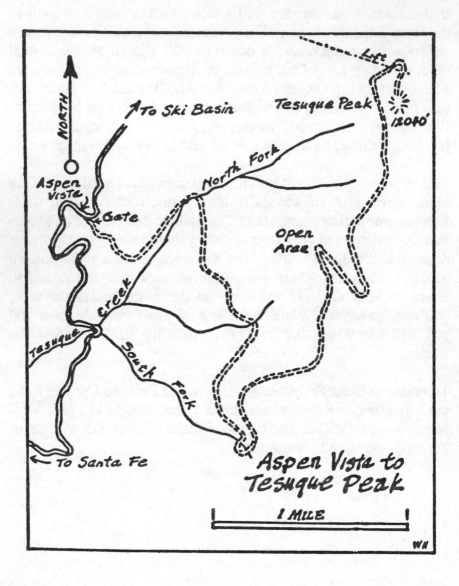

NORTH

To Ski Basin

Tesuque Peak

12,040'

Lift

Aspen Vista

Gate

North Fork

Open Area

Tesuque

Creek

South Fork

To Santa Fe

Aspen Vista to Tesuque Peak

1 MILE

WN

ASPEN VISTA TO TESUQUE PEAK

by
Walt Kunz

U.S. GEOLOGICAL SURVEY MAP REQUIRED: Aspen Basin
- 7.5 minute series. The 1977 topo map shows the road on which
you will be walking. A 'Visitor's Guide to the Pecos Wilderness'
also shows the road, and is available from the Forest Service.

SALIENT FEATURES: Good stands of aspen, spruce and fir,
clear streams, large open areas with excellent views. Trail is a dirt
road. Especially beautiful in the fall when the aspens are golden.
This is a popular and often crowded area at the height of the aspen
viewing in late September and early October.

RATING: Easy to strenuous, depending on the distance traveled.

ROUND TRIP HIKING DISTANCE: 12 miles for the entire hike,
but can be made any length you choose.

APPROXIMATE ROUND TRIP HIKING TIME: 6 hours for the
entire hike.

ALTITUDE RANGE: Highest point, 12,040 feet; lowest point,
10,000 feet; cumulative uphill hiking for the entire hike, 2040 feet.

SEASONAL CONSIDERATIONS: Usually snowed in at higher
altitudes in winter and spring, and popular with cross country

skiers in the winter. Even in July you may encounter snow. Bring adequate clothing.

ROUND TRIP DRIVING: 27 miles; approximately one hour.

DRIVING DIRECTIONS: From the plaza, drive north on Washington Avenue 6 blocks and turn right on Artist Road. There is a sign here pointing to Hyde State Park and the Ski Basin. Measure your mileage from the turn. Drive 12.6 miles, then turn right into a large parking lot marked by a large sign for Aspen Vista.

HIKING INSTRUCTIONS: There is a gated access road on the east side of the parking area which is the start of the trail to Tesuque Peak. The "not for public use" sign refers to vehicles only; hiking (as well as cross country skiing) is permitted. This is the service road for the microwave relay station at the peak.

The first 2.5 miles are through aspen forest (spectacular in the fall); the last 3.5 miles are through fir and spruce alternating with large treeless areas. About 0.5/mile in you can catch a glimpse of your destination, the bare peak with microwave towers straight ahead. At 0.8/mile you cross the north fork of Big Tesuque Creek, at 1.6 miles, two more forks of the creek, and at 2.3 miles, the last fork. Water-loving flowers abound along the banks of the creeks. Late in the summer the lower stretches of the road are lined with masses of yellow senecio and purple asters.

Just past the last creek crossing, the road makes a switchback to the north (left) and enters a fir and spruce forest. At 3.8 miles the road traverses a large open area which affords good views of the Rio Grande valley north of Santa Fe, and, a bit farther along, a panoramic view of Santa Fe.

On your left you will see a large outcropping of rock which makes a good rest area and a turnaround point if you don't want to hike the entire distance.

At 5 miles, after a few more switchbacks, the road turns northeast and enters the forest again. (This section has had 3 feet of snow across the road in mid-July.) At 5.5 miles the road enters another large open area. Below, to the northwest, you can see the top of a chair lift at the Santa Fe Ski Basin. The long fence straight ahead is a snow fence along one of the ski trails served by the ski lifts under which you will pass farther up the road. Above, to the northeast, are the microwave towers on Tesuque Peak, about half a mile away by road.

At the top, the terrain drops steeply eastward into the Santa Fe River valley, a closed area which provides a main part of Santa Fe's water supply. To the north is Lake Peak, about a mile away.

Return by the same route.

An alternate return route, with another car having been shuttled to and left at the Santa Fe Ski Basin, is to take one of the ski trails (if you know the trails) down to the ski basin parking lot. This maneuver would increase considerably the steepness of the descent but would shorten the hike by approximately 4 miles.

Fastest round trip time by runners is about one and a quarter hours.

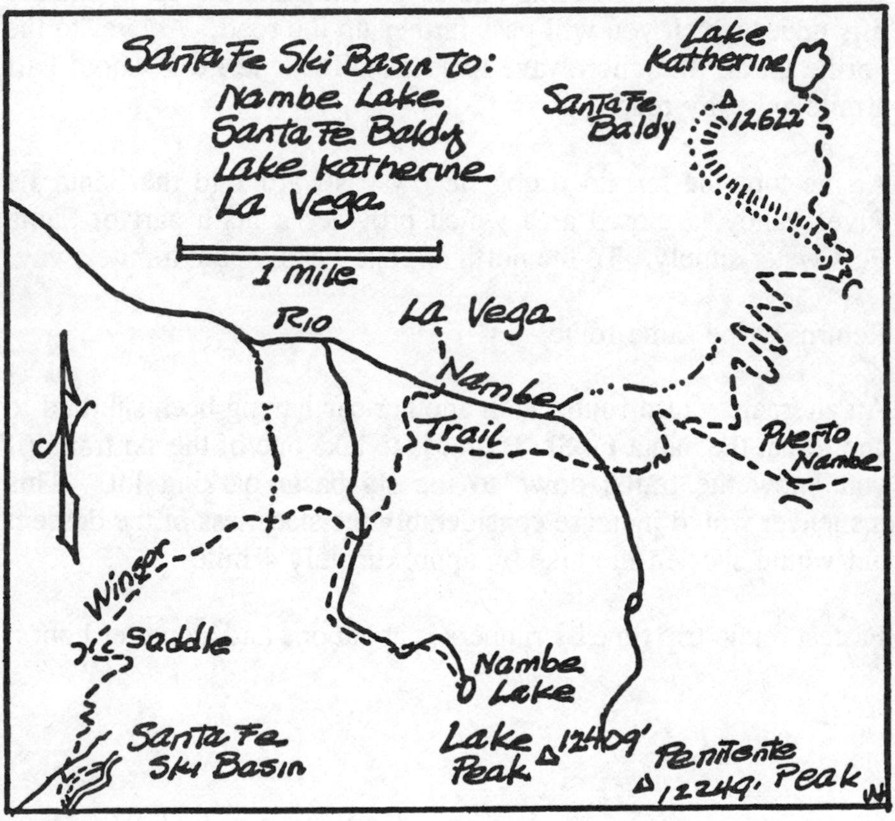

Santa Fe Ski Basin to:
Nambe Lake
Santa Fe Baldy
Lake Katherine
La Vega

Lake Katherine

Santa Fe Baldy   △ 12,622'

1 mile

Rio   La Vega

Nambe

Trail

Puerto Nambe

Winsor

Saddle

Nambe Lake

Santa Fe Ski Basin

Lake Peak   △ 12,409'   Penitente Peak
                          △ 12,249'

40

NAMBÉ LAKE

by
Carolyn Keskulla

U.S. GEOLOGICAL SURVEY MAP REQUIRED: Aspen Basin - 7.5 minute series. This trail is not shown on the topo map, but does appear on the Pecos Wilderness map available at US Forest Service headquarters. See sketch map on page 40.

SALIENT FEATURES: You will have the special treat of seeing Nambé Lake, which nestles under the cliff face of Lake Peak. Good hiking shoes are a necessity as the trail is very steep and in some places rocky as it climbs alongside Nambé Creek.

RATING: Moderate in distance, but there are some steep, rocky climbs.

ROUND TRIP HIKING DISTANCE: 7 miles.

APPROXIMATE ROUND TRIP HIKING TIME: About 5 hours, allowing time for lunch and a stroll around the lake.

ALTITUDE RANGE: Highest point, 11,400 feet; lowest point, 10,260 feet; cumulative uphill hiking, 2100 feet.

SEASONAL CONSIDERATIONS: Generally accessible from mid-June to first heavy snow; may be snowed-in at other times.

ROUND TRIP DRIVING: 30 miles; 1 hour 20 minutes.

DRIVING DIRECTIONS: From the plaza, drive north on Washington Avenue 6 blocks and turn right on Artist Road. There is a sign here pointing to Hyde State Park and the Ski Basin. Measure your mileage from the turn. Continue 14 miles to the Ski Basin and, at the Ski Basin, keep to the left and park in the lower parking lot. Look for a sign that says, "WINSOR TRAIL."

HIKING INSTRUCTIONS: After crossing the small wooden bridge, turn right and start uphill on the well-used Winsor Trail #254. After a half mile or more of steep climbing you will be at the wilderness boundary fence, 560 feet higher than the trailhead. Watch for the lovely wildflowers among the aspen and spruce. In June you may see shooting star and fairy slipper orchid. From the fence you start gently downhill passing, in about a quarter of a mile, a little noticed trail on the left. This is a very steep trail to the Rio Nambé nicknamed the "elevator shaft." Continue past it for about two miles from the start.

You will come to a clearing on your right. Ahead of you, the Winsor Trail drops down to cross the Nambé Lake Creek. Look for a trail going up to the right (south) alongside this lovely cascading alpine stream. There is no officially maintained trail to Nambé Lake, which is hidden behind the high ridge to the southeast, but, over the years, hikers have consistently used the easiest way up the stream to the lake. There are several paths, all of which will eventually lead you to the lake. By using your own instinct and following the course of the stream and the paths, you will reach the lake, the source of the Rio Nambé. The easiest route is to follow the well-worn trail up on either side of the stream at first, then stay on the left bank. Keep the stream within earshot as you climb steeply. The lake will eventually appear surrounded by spruce forest and talus slopes.

The shallow lake nestles under the cliff face of Lake Peak. Flowers grow in profusion in July along the stream and around the lake. Parry's primrose, mertensia, and marsh marigold are spectacular in early July. Later there will be fireweed, yampa, monkshood and many others. You may also see marmots and pika scampering around the slopes.

Return by the same route.

LA VEGA

by
Norbert Sperlich

U.S. GEOLOGICAL SURVEY MAP REQUIRED: Aspen Basin - 7.5 minute series. How to locate La Vega on the topo map? Find the Ski Area first, called "Santa Fe Recreation Area" on the map. Now find Aspen Peak (northwest of the Ski Area) and Santa Fe Baldy (northeast of the Ski Area). Place a ruler over the tops of Aspen Peak and Santa Fe Baldy. Starting at Santa Fe Baldy, follow the ruler down for 4 inches. You will come to a level area, indicated by the absence of contour lines. This is La Vega, Spanish for "meadow" or "pasture land." See sketch map on page 40.

SALIENT FEATURES: This hike through aspen, fir, and spruce takes you to an open meadow at the foot of Santa Fe Baldy. La Vega offers a beautiful setting away from the sometimes crowded Winsor Trail. Many wildflowers in season. Spectacular in late September and early October, when the aspens are golden.

RATING: Moderate.

ROUND TRIP HIKING DISTANCE: Approximately 7 miles.

APPROXIMATE ROUND TRIP HIKING TIME: 3 to 4 hours.

ALTITUDE RANGE: Highest point, 10,840 feet; lowest point, 10,000 feet; cumulative uphill hiking, approximately 1500 feet.

SEASONAL CONSIDERATIONS: Do not attempt this hike in snow.

ROUND TRIP DRIVING: 30 miles; about 1 hour 20 minutes.

DRIVING DIRECTIONS: From the plaza, drive north on Washington Avenue 6 blocks and turn right on Artist Road. There is a sign here pointing to Hyde State Park and the Ski Basin. Measure your mileage from here. Continue uphill 14 miles to the Ski Basin and, at the Ski Basin, keep to the left and park in the lower parking lot. Look for a sign that says, "WINSOR TRAIL."

HIKING INSTRUCTIONS: From the trailhead, you will cross a small stream and go up on the Winsor Trail (to the right, Trail #254). The trail zigzags up through a forest of aspen, fir, and spruce trees and crosses several small meadows. After half an hour or so of steep climbing you come to a meadow and the entrance gate to the Pecos Wilderness. You have reached the highest point of the hike (10,840 feet). Time to catch your breath and to feed the gray jays that are usually waiting here for handouts from hikers.

The trail now descends gradually through stands of conifers and aspens. After about an hour of hiking time (from the Ski Basin) you will reach a clearing to the right of the trail. Just before the clearing, a smaller trail goes off to the right to Nambé Lake. (See page 41 for a description of the hike to Nambé Lake.) You will continue straight ahead on the Winsor Trail which, right after the clearing, crosses Nambé Creek. Check the time at this point. In about five minutes you will reach the turnoff to La Vega, a small trail that goes down to the left. Look for a sign on the right side of the trail. The sign says:

UPPER NAMBE TRAIL 101
RIO NAMBE
LA VEGA

Here, you leave the well-traveled Winsor Trail and take the trail to La Vega. This trail is not on the topo map!

For a while, the trail stays on top of a ridge, then it drops down into the valley to the right of the ridge. Keep your eyes on the trail. It is overgrown in some places and obstructed by fallen aspen trees in others. At the valley bottom, the trail enters a conifer forest and then comes to a stream (a tributary of the Nambé River). At this point, you have hiked for about 20 minutes on the La Vega Shortcut Trail. You have now reached the lowest point of the hike (approximately 10,000 feet). Cross the stream on a bridge of slippery logs. The trail now turns left and goes up on the other side of the creek. About 30 yards away from the stream, your trail merges with Trail #160 (Rio Nambé Trail). The junction is marked by a signpost with two signs. One of them points in the direction from which you came; the other sign, indicating the Rio Nambé Trail, says "Trail 160." You take the left branch of the latter trail. For a while, the trail descends slowly, with the stream on your left within earshot. After a few minutes, you will be going uphill again and the trail moves to the right, away from the stream. Some 10 minutes after passing the last sign (near the creek), the trail will take you up to a low ridge. Ahead of you is a clearing and a signpost. The sign, about chest high (likely to be destroyed by vandals) will tell you:

LA VEGA
← RIO NAMBÉ TRAIL
← BORREGO TRAIL 4
← ASPEN RANCH 7

The trail is not clearly visible beyond this point. Walk 10 yards or so past the signpost, and you will look down on La Vega, a large meadow (altitude about 10,100 feet) interspersed with spruce and fir trees and patches of gooseberry bushes. Opposite you, to the north, the meadow is framed by two ridges that lead up to Santa Fe Baldy. (The top of Santa Fe Baldy is not visible from this point.)

A little stream comes down in the valley between the two ridges and meanders through the meadow, turning to the west to join Nambé Creek further down. If you are lucky, you might see deer bounding across the meadow. More likely, you will encounter a herd of grazing cattle.

Before you move on to explore La Vega or to relax at the bank of the stream, memorize the location of the LA VEGA signpost. You will have to return to this post in order to find the trail. When exploring the meadow, watch out for swampy areas.

Start your return at the sign post and go back the way you came. After a few minutes of hiking you will hear the creek below you on the right. Once the creek comes into your view, watch for the turnoff to the right and the sign on the left side of the trail. Turn to the right and go down to the stream. Cross the stream and retrace your steps back to the Winsor Trail. When you reach the Winsor Trail, turn right and go back to the Ski Basin.

SANTA FE BALDY

by
Arnold and Carolyn Keskulla

U.S. GEOLOGICAL SURVEY MAP REQUIRED: Aspen Basin - 7.5 minute series. See sketch map on page 40.

SALIENT FEATURES: You will experience the satisfaction of achieving the summit of a beautiful mountain with unsurpassed views and lovely wildflowers. There are steep grades and high altitudes. Pick a clear day to make your climb and be well equipped with full canteen, poncho, lunch and energy. This is a strenuous hike and you should be in good shape. Start as early as you can in order to be off the peak before the usual summer afternoon thunderstorms begin.

RATING: Strenuous.

ROUND TRIP HIKING DISTANCE: 13 to 14 miles.

APPROXIMATE ROUND TRIP HIKING TIME: 8 hours.

ALTITUDE RANGE: Highest point, 12,622 feet; lowest point, 10,260 feet; cumulative uphill hiking, 2760 feet.

SEASONAL CONSIDERATIONS: Generally accessible from mid-June to mid-September. The best time to climb Santa Fe Baldy is in late June or early July because the thunderstorm season

48

may not have begun and the forget-me-nots and other alpine flowers are in profusion.

ROUND TRIP DRIVING: 30 miles; approximately 1 hour 20 minutes.

DRIVING DIRECTIONS: From the plaza, drive north on Washington Avenue 6 blocks and turn right on Artist Road. There is a sign here pointing to Hyde State Park and the Ski Basin. Measure your mileage from the turn. Continue uphill 14 miles to the Ski Basin and, at the Ski Basin, keep to the left and park in the lower parking lot. Look for a sign that says, "WINSOR TRAIL."

HIKING INSTRUCTIONS: After crossing the small wooden bridge turn right and start uphill on the well-used Winsor Trail, #254. In a half mile or more of steep climbing you will be at the wilderness boundary fence, 560 feet higher than the trailhead. Watch for the lovely wildflowers among the aspen and spruce. In June you may see shooting star and fairy slipper orchid. From the fence you start gently downhill, passing in about a quarter of a mile a little-noticed trail on the left. This is a very steep trail to the Rio Nambé nicknamed the "elevator shaft." Continue past it for about two miles from the start. Here a trail goes south up to lovely Nambé Lake beneath Lake Peak (see page 41 for the Nambé Lake hike). However, you go straight ahead across the Rio Nambé and continue along the Winsor Trail. After crossing two streams (which feed into the Rio Nambé), start up the switchbacks which will lead you to a trail junction at 11,000 feet, 4.5 miles from the Ski Basin. The level grassy meadow here is generally referred to as Puerto Nambé.

Take the left fork, Trail #251 (not shown on the U.S.G.S. map) which leaves the Winsor Trail and goes northeasterly up long switchbacks to the top of a saddle. From the saddle leave the trail and strike for the summit up the ridge to your left (north) by line of sight. There is a rough trail near the edge of the ridge.

This is a steep ascent, so you may have to make your own switchbacks and rest occasionally. There may be a few snow patches. Along with your lunch, enjoy the superb views from the top, and don't miss looking down on Lake Katherine by walking a short distance to the northeast. The unforgettable blue forget-me-nots, fairy primroses, sky pilots and other beautiful alpine flowers will be abundant early in the season. Later, bistorts, gentians, composites and others will appear. You have climbed to the summit of a 12,622 foot peak, a memorable experience!

Remember to turn back at any sign of a thunderstorm. Before you leave the top, check your bearings by sight or compass so that you can reach Puerto Nambé and the trail back to the ski basin. Don't try to take a shortcut down; rather, return by the same route you ascended. Many hikers have gotten themselves lost by trying to take a shortcut back to the Winsor Trail.

LAKE KATHERINE

by
Kenneth D. Adam

U.S. GEOLOGICAL SURVEY MAPS REQUIRED: Aspen Basin and Cowles - 7.5 minute series. The current maps do not show the trail from Puerto Nambé to Lake Katherine, but the Pecos Wilderness Map from the Forest Service does. See sketch map, page 40.

SALIENT FEATURES: A high altitude hike over well-marked trails through aspen, fir and spruce forest and high alpine meadows, ending in a beautiful alpine lake in a spectacular setting. Fine views of nearby peaks and distant valleys.

RATING: Strenuous.

ROUND TRIP HIKING DISTANCE: 14.5 miles.

APPROXIMATE ROUND TRIP HIKING TIME: 7-8 hours, plus stops.

ALTITUDE RANGE: Highest point, 11,750 feet; lowest point, 10,250 feet; cumulative uphill hiking, 3200 feet.

SEASONAL CONSIDERATIONS: Practical from about early June, depending on snow, until the first major snowfall.

ROUND TRIP DRIVING: 30 miles; approximately 1 hour 20 minutes.

51

DRIVING DIRECTIONS: From the plaza, drive north on Washington Avenue 6 blocks and turn right on Artist Road. There is a sign here pointing to Hyde State Park and the Ski Basin. Measure your mileage from the turn. Continue 14 miles to the Ski Basin and, at the Ski Basin, keep to the left and park in the lower parking lot. Look for a sign that says, "WINSOR TRAIL."

HIKING INSTRUCTIONS: From the trailhead, immediately cross a small stream (the upper part of the Rio en Medio), turn right and start to climb. The trail starts with the steepest climb of the day through mixed aspen and conifer forest (very spectacular in the fall). After two or three switchbacks and a couple of small meadows (wild iris in season), you will arrive at the entrance gate of the Pecos Wilderness in a meadow at the top of the first climb. This pass is between the watersheds of the Rio en Medio and Rio Nambé. The elevation here is 10,850 feet.

The trail now traverses the north slope of the divide, gradually losing altitude for about 1.5 miles until it reaches a sparkling stream, Nambé Creek. You will have been walking about one hour at this point. The trail continues to traverse, without much altitude change, to the northeast. Keep to the main (Winsor) trail, #254, now climbing slightly through aspen groves and small meadows. You will cross three minor streams and pass by two places where trails lead off to the left from the main trail. Stay on the main trail, Winsor Creek Trail #254. The three-quarters of a mile uphill stretch from the last stream to Puerto Nambé will seem more like a mile. After twenty or twenty-five minutes you will finally reach the "Y" trail junction at Puerto Nambé in a beautiful high meadow. There are fine views of Santa Fe Baldy to the north and Lake Peak and Penitente Peak to the south and southeast. While you stop to rest at the junction, several gray jays will probably pester you for a handout. With just a little patience on your part, they will eat from your hand.

You now leave the Winsor Creek Trail and take Sky Line Trail, the left trail at the "Y." From here on, the trail is not shown on the U.S.G.S. topo map. It crosses the meadow and starts up a series of long, long switchbacks which finally bring you to the divide between the Rio Nambé and Pecos watersheds. You will have been walking about three hours at this point. This is a wonderful rest/snack spot with dramatic scenery in all directions: the upper Pecos basin to the east, the Rio Grande valley and Jemez Mountains to the west, Santa Fe Baldy right next to you on the northwest and Lake Peak and Penitente Peak to the south and southeast.

You are at the edge of a steep dropoff to the east, and looking down you can see your trail zigging and zagging down in a series of seven switchbacks. After dropping down these switchbacks, the trail starts a climbing traverse to the northwest across the upper edge of a large talus slope, then through open forest. Level stretches of trail are interrupted with short climbs up switchbacks. Be on the look-out for abrupt changes in trail direction that mark switchbacks. You finally leave the forest and cross an open talus-covered area. The trail is not very definite here. At the end of the talus area is a sign reading "Lake Katherine," although you cannot yet see the lake. A short walk through open forest brings you to the eastern shoreline of Lake Katherine, elevation 11,742 feet.

You are in a high alpine bowl, with Santa Fe Baldy directly above you to the southwest. The peak is so close that you may be tempted to climb it on your way home. This can be done by climbing the steep grassy slope above the west shore of the lake and following the ridge to the summit. It involves an extra 900 feet of climbing at high altitude, however, and is emphatically not recommended unless every member of your party is in excellent shape and you know your way back from the summit.

The recommended return is by retracing your route in reverse.

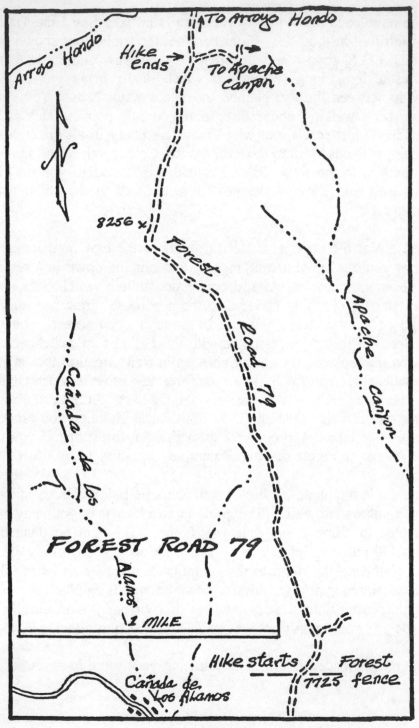

FOREST SERVICE ROAD #79

by
Wesley Horner

U.S. GEOLOGICAL SURVEY MAPS REQUIRED: Glorieta and McClure Reservoir - 7.5 minute series.

SALIENT FEATURES: A pleasant road walk within the Santa Fe National Forest in the foothills near Santa Fe, with gentle grades, following a long ridge covered with spring and summer wildflowers and open ponderosa pine woods providing excellent views in every direction.

RATING: Easy.

ROUND TRIP HIKING DISTANCE: 5.5 miles.

APPROXIMATE ROUND TRIP HIKING TIME: 2½-3 hours.

ALTITUDE RANGE: Highest point, 8260 feet; lowest point, 7700 feet; cumulative uphill hiking, 560 feet.

SEASONAL CONSIDERATIONS: Year-round hike.

ROUND TRIP DRIVING: 24 miles; one hour.

DRIVING DIRECTIONS: From downtown Santa Fe, drive south on Old Santa Fe Trail, which becomes Old Pecos Trail, to the stop light at the intersection of Rodeo Road and the Old Las Vegas way with Old Pecos Trail. At the light take a left turn onto Old Las Vegas Highway. About 3 miles from the light look for a brown sign indicating the turn-off to Camp Stoney. Turn left here. Once on this road, which is Santa Fe County Road #67C, you may see a Forest Road 79 sign. (At this point you are approximately 5 miles from the start of the hike.) Go 0.9/mile to a "T" intersection. Turn right, following the main County Road #67 about 2.2 miles to a "Y" where the pavement ends and the Camp Stoney road goes straight ahead. Take the left hand fork (County Road #67A) down the hill to and through the village of Cañada de los Alamos. About a quarter of a mile past the blue-roofed church, you will cross the first cattle guard and then head downhill. Continue along the road, which at times serves as a stream bed, following it as it curves left sharply uphill. Bear left at the top of the hill after the third cattle guard where the road splits. Pass the Santa Fe Treehouse Camp (SFTHC) on your right, a short distance beyond which is the Forest Boundary at the fourth cattle guard, where the hike begins.

There is ample parking space on the left before crossing the cattle guard, or on the right after crossing it.

HIKING INSTRUCTIONS: Immediately past the cattle guard, bear left. (The right-hand fork goes to the private Apache Creek development.) As the road follows an open ridge it affords fine views in all directions. To the east, on your right, is the aptly-named Shaggy Peak, showing bold outcrops of pre-Cambrian granite and gneiss. The same rock forms the ridge and underlies the surrounding area. On the skyline behind is a high ridge whose two prominent summits are Glorieta Baldy and, farther to the north, Thompson Peak. In the far distance to the northeast are the higher peaks of the Sangre de Cristo Range, snow-patched during most of the year. To the southwest lie the low foothills of the Cerros Negros, and beyond are the Ortiz Mountains and the Cerrillos Hills, where gold and turquoise, respectively, have been mined for centuries. On the far horizon are the Sandias, standing just east of Albuquerque, and more toward the west Mount Taylor, an isolated volcanic pile, over a hundred miles away.

The walk is made especially pleasant by the easy footing and by the ponderosa pine forest through which the road passes. Selective timber cutting has opened the woods for the continued healthy growth of those trees left, as well as for the numerous new ones. There is little underbrush, so the needle carpet forms a smooth gray cover on the forest floor. Since the ridge is high and open, the wind is usually whispering through the pines. You will pass a few side roads leading to Forest Service inholdings or private property; keep to the main road.

The highest point in the hike is reached about 2 miles from the start where the elevation is 8256 feet, marked by the USGS benchmark HONDO, a low square concrete pillar topped with a brass marker, standing about 20 feet off the road to the left. Here the road curves to the right and continues to follow the ridge for about another half mile to the turn-around point of the hike, marked by a sign which says "Dead End Road." The mountain straight ahead is Sierra Pelada. The dead end Forest Service road leads over into Apache Canyon about two miles north. The faint narrow road on the left goes down into the head of Arroyo Hondo.

At the high point on your return to your car you will see in the distance to the southeast vast waves of gently southward-sloping high mesas, formed by Mesozoic sandstone and shale strata, marking the southern end of the Sangre de Cristo uplift.

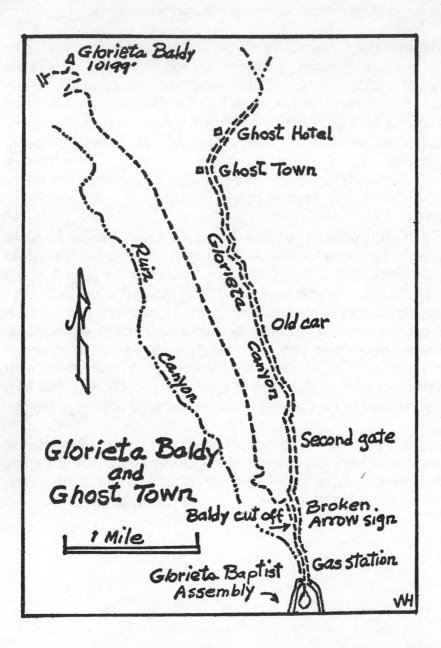

Glorieta Baldy
10199'

Ghost Hotel

Ghost Town

Ruiz Canyon

Glorieta Canyon

Old car

Second gate

Glorieta Baldy
and
Ghost Town

1 Mile

Baldy cut off

Broken.
Arrow sign

Glorieta Baptist
Assembly

Gas station

VH

58

GLORIETA BALDY

by
Bill Chudd

U.S. GEOLOGICAL SURVEY MAPS REQUIRED: Glorieta and McClure Reservoir - 7.5 minute series. Caution -- there is a trail shown on these maps which is not the current trail and which took an entirely different route to the summit. The present trail is not shown. It approaches the summit along a ridge between Glorieta Canyon to the east and Ruiz Canyon to the west. At this writing, a map prepared by the U.S.G.S. and the Safety-Security Unit of the Glorieta Conference Center is available at the trailhead. The upper trail is not shown in detail as to the final switchbacks and approach to the lookout tower.

SALIENT FEATURES: Easy approach on paved roads to the wilderness trailhead. A steady uphill trail, quite steep in places, to a 10,200 foot peak with a fire lookout tower. Intimations of heaven and sweeping views of earth. Downhill all the way back. Carry sufficient water.

RATING: Strenuous.

ROUND TRIP HIKING DISTANCE: Rated at 10.2 miles on the map provided at the trailhead and at 14 miles on the sign near the trailhead. My estimate: 11 steep, strenuous, and satisfying miles.

APPROXIMATE ROUND TRIP HIKING TIME: 6 hours; roughly 3½ hours up, 2¼ hours down. Due to the steady, steep ascent, the time will vary according to the condition of the hikers.

ALTITUDE RANGE: Highest point, 10,199 feet; lowest point, 7475 feet; cumulative uphill hiking, 2800 feet.

SEASONAL CONSIDERATIONS: An excellent spring, summer and fall walk. The early part of the trail may be hard to follow when snow-covered. Likely to be heavily snowed-in in midwinter. In summer start early enough to be off the peak shortly after noon to avoid the afternoon lightning storms. Carry a flashlight in all seasons; the Director of the Maintenance Department at the Conference Center says that 20-30 people get lost on this trail every summer.

ROUND TRIP DRIVING: 40 miles; about an hour.

DRIVING DIRECTIONS: From Santa Fe, take I-25 toward Las Vegas, New Mexico, to exit #299 at Glorieta. Following the direction signs for the Glorieta Baptist Conference Center, turn left at the top of the ramp. At the barrier, turn left again, paralleling the highway, to the gatehouse of the Conference Center. Stop at the gatehouse and if there is a security officer there advise him or her of your hike plan.

On leaving the gatehouse, immediately turn right onto Oak Street. Follow Oak Street through the conference grounds. At 0.6/mile from the gate, Oak Street turns right. Do not go straight ahead, a move which would mislead you onto Willow Street, but continue on Oak Street to the right. There is a small street sign at this street fork. At 0.9/mile, you will see a bicycle/ski rental shop (the old firehouse) on the right. Park here.

HIKING INSTRUCTIONS: Walk further on Oak Street about 100 feet to the first intersection, with Holly Street. There are signs at this intersection: a high "Shell" sign on the left of the side street and a "Service Station - Hiking Trails" sign on the right. Turn right onto the side street. In about 200 yards, after leaving the pavement and continuing on the dirt road, you will come to a fence with a trail register at the left of the road. Register your hike, pick up a trail map if available, and continue along the road. In another 200 yards you will see a prominent sign pointing out the trail to Broken Arrow and Glorieta Baldy on your left and to Ghost Town straight ahead. Leave the road, turning onto the trail to your left.

Follow this trail uphill and to the left where it levels off among large boulders and seems to end. White arrows painted on the rocks and later on trees will direct you to your right, over the boulders, to the continuation of the trail. Study this area carefully. It is easy to get lost here on the return trip. After crossing the boulders, you may see the ribbon trail markers that the Maintenance Department places at close intervals each spring to help hikers find the main trail among the many paths that have been made by Conference Center visitors. In a short time, you will come to a wooden gate, where the trail is much clearer.

The trail makes a number of small switchbacks and keeps climbing, with nice views toward the west (on your left). In the distance, behind a ridge, you will be able to identify the top of Shaggy Peak. Shortly, you will reach the top of a ridge, a good place to get your bearings. Eastward, to your right, you will be looking down into Glorieta Canyon. Westward, to your left, is a side canyon out of Ruiz Canyon. You are just above the mouth of this canyon which continues northward for a while between you and Ruiz. The trail follows the top of the ridge, climbing very gently.

About 2 miles into the hike you will see a trail merging in from the right with a sign, "Trail Closed." Continue straight ahead. After this junction the trail widens and becomes progressively steeper. The ridge, too, widens until you are simply climbing up a hillside. You may still be able to spot old blazes and white or orange

61

painted blaze markers on some tree trunks. After a long, gentle climb, the trail becomes much steeper until it narrows and turns downhill for several hundred feet to cross a drainage ravine (the upper portion of Ruiz Canyon). After crossing the ravine, the trail turns left and goes steeply upward on the right side of the drainage bed.

The ponderosa pines have given way to firs and, at about 9500 feet, patches of aspen appear. These will announce themselves with shouting golden hues in late September and October. From time to time you will get dramatic views back toward Glorieta and an occasional view of the lookout tower ahead through the tree tops.

The slope becomes increasingly steep and the trail begins to switch back and forth across a runoff channel which is often used by hikers as the trail. Should you get onto this channel and find yourself climbing directly skyward, continue until you intersect the next trail switchback. There are small orange flags (the type used for buried cable or pipe) here and there along the switchbacks. If these are maintained they will help you stay on the trail.

A few hundred feet from the lookout tower a trail comes in from the left. Turn right and proceed to the base of the tower. Before making the turn note this junction well and when starting down be sure you do not miss the left turn back onto the trail you came up.

Look around. Wasn't it worth it? I've sat here on a day with broken clouds rolling below, revealing glimpses of hilltops, mesas and distant plains, as though looking down from heaven. On another unheavenly, still day with a temperature inversion, I looked to the southwest to see Albuquerque smog snaking around the north slopes of Sandia Mountain and sending a gray-brown plume out over the plains to the east. It's an ever-changing, always remarkable view.

Descend by the same trail. When you reach the lower, flatter
of the ridge where yucca and other dry plants grow, it is easy to
misled by the many trails that lead off from campfire rings and
campsites. Look for the trail that you came up on on the right
(east), with its switchbacks down the hill.

When you get back to the Conference Center, you may wish to
explore this curious city in the wilderness. From your parking
area, you may choose to continue driving further on Oak Street,
which completes a circle of the Conference Center grounds and
returns you to the entrance gate.

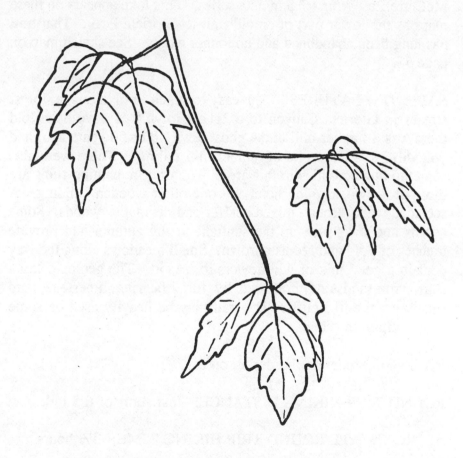

GLORIETA GHOST TOWN

by
Bill Chudd

U.S. GEOLOGICAL SURVEY MAPS REQUIRED: Glorieta and McClure Reservoir - 7.5 minute series. This hike appears on these maps as the lower part of an old trail to Glorieta Peak. That trail has long been abandoned and no longer exists. See sketch map on page 58.

SALIENT FEATURES: An easy-to-reach trail along a forest stream in Glorieta Canyon to a "ghost town." I have been told there was a lumber mill at the ghost town 40 or 50 years ago, and you will see a large pile of lumber mill tailings. There were also some mining activities in this area. The only remaining ruins are those of a two-story log hotel and one other wooden building. A secluded walk through mixed conifer and deciduous woods. Some aspens and oaks pick up the sunlight in the autumn and provide touches of gold and reddish brown. Small meadows along the way contain a good mix of wildflowers in season. The geologic strata start with sandstone, followed by fossil-bearing limestone, and finally granite-like cliffs. The trail may be heavily used on some days, empty on others.

RATING: Moderate, bordering on easy.

ROUND TRIP HIKING DISTANCE: Just short of 6.5 miles.

APPROXIMATE ROUND TRIP HIKING TIME: 3½ hours.

ALTITUDE RANGE: Highest point, 8420 feet; lowest point, 7475 feet; cumulative uphill hiking, 950 feet.

SEASONAL CONSIDERATIONS: This can be an all-year walk, although accessibility in winter will depend on the amount of snowfall. The stream flow varies widely with the seasons. It may present difficult crossings at the height of the spring runoff or may be completely dry after prolonged drought.

ROUND TRIP DRIVING: 40 miles; one hour.

DRIVING DIRECTIONS: From Santa Fe, take I-25 toward Las Vegas, New Mexico, to exit #299 at Glorieta. Following the direction signs for the Glorieta Baptist Conference Center, turn left at the top of the ramp. At the barrier, turn left again, paralleling the highway, to the gatehouse of the Conference Center. Stop at the gatehouse and, if there is a security officer there, advise him or her of your hike plan.

On leaving the gatehouse, immediately turn right onto Oak Street. Follow Oak Street through the conference grounds. At 0.6/mile from the gate, Oak Street turns right. Do not go straight ahead, a move which would mislead you onto Willow Street, but continue on Oak Street to the right. There is a small street sign at this street fork. At 0.9/mile, you will see a bicycle/ski rental shop (the old firehouse) on the right. Park here.

HIKING INSTRUCTIONS: Continue on Oak Street about 100 feet to the first intersection, with Holly Street. There are signs at this intersection: a high "Shell" sign on the left of the side street and a "Service Station - Hiking Trails" sign on the right. Turn right onto the side street. In about 200 yards, after leaving the pavement and continuing on the dirt road, you will reach a fence with a trail register at the left of the road. After registering your hike, continue along the road. Soon you will reach a sign marking the turnoff to the left to Broken Arrow and Glorieta Baldy. Stay straight ahead to Ghost Town. If you are unsure about your route, follow alongside the stream.

Many of the common local wildflowers can be seen beside the road on the early part of the walk. About a half mile in, you will come to a fence with an open field beyond. The field has a heavy growth of mullein and also some yellow or yellow and brown prairie coneflowers, not too common in our area.

Beyond the field, just before the road turns toward the right, you will again be reassured by a sign pointing back toward the trailhead and ahead to Ghost Town. You will now be walking along what remains of the road to the old "Ghost Hotel." It climbs gradually. While the ascent totals about 900 feet, there are no really steep parts. The good news is that it's downhill all the way back.

You will begin to notice a small stream roughly paralleling the trail. It will stay with you all the way but here and there will take off for a little while, probably to get you to appreciate it more when it returns. You will cross the stream from time to time and, in places where it has eroded the road, take streamside paths or even walk 20 or 30 feet in the stream itself. The water is usually quite shallow.

At about three miles the first of the two ruins, that of an old wooden building, will appear on your left. Here the trail narrows to a thin path through the meadow between the ruin and the stream, then broadens again to the width of a primitive road. In less than a half mile you will reach another meadow. The ridge to your right across the stream features towering cliffs. Ahead and to your left, at the northwest end of the field, is your destination, "Ghost Hotel."

You may want to explore a bit of the surrounding area. Beyond the hotel ruin, toward the northwest, if you follow a barely visible path for about 100 feet or more, you will come to the entrance of an old mineshaft carved into the hillside rock on the right side of a small canyon. When I was last there, the floor of the mine was flooded. After your exploration, sit a while. Enjoy a snack. Looking at the cliffs to the east, across the stream, imagine, as I did, a colorful sunrise over these hills at the time the Ghost Hotel was in its heyday.

Upon your return to the parking area, you may choose to continue driving further on Oak Street, which completes a circle of the Conference Center grounds and returns you to the entrance gate.

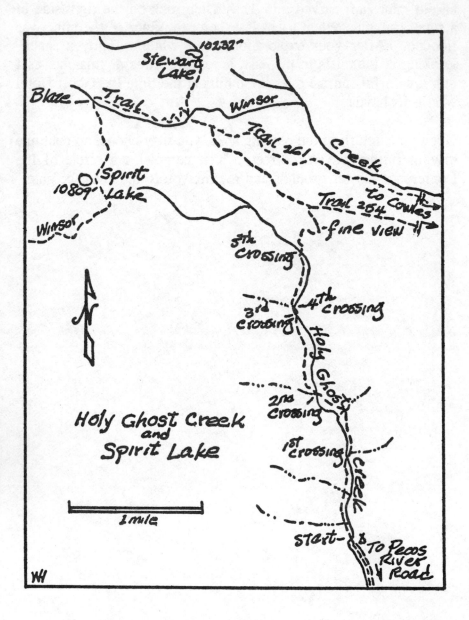

Holy Ghost Creek
and
Spirit Lake

1 mile

WH

HOLY GHOST CREEK AND SPIRIT LAKE
(The Espiritu Santo Walk)

by
Carl Overhage

U.S. GEOLOGICAL SURVEY MAP REQUIRED: Cowles - 7.5 minute series.

SALIENT FEATURES: An uphill walk through flowering meadows, aspen groves, spruce forest, past a cascading stream, to a lovely mountain lake.

RATING: Strenuous.

ROUND TRIP HIKING DISTANCE: 14 miles.

APPROXIMATE ROUND TRIP HIKING TIME: 9 hours.

ALTITUDE RANGE: Highest point, 10,800 feet; lowest point, 8150 feet; cumulative uphill hiking, 2750 feet.

SEASONAL CONSIDERATIONS: Summer and fall until the first snow. Early in the season, the stream crossings may be difficult due to snow melt.

ROUND TRIP DRIVING: 81 miles; approximately 3 hours.

DRIVING DIRECTIONS: From Santa Fe take I-25 toward Las Vegas, New Mexico, for approximately 15 miles and exit on the

Glorieta off-ramp #299. Turn left on the overpass, then turn right on State Road #50 and drive 6 miles to the town of Pecos. At the stop sign turn left onto State Road #63, which leads north into the Pecos River valley. Measure your mileage from this stop sign. Drive 13.5 miles to the Terrero bridge. Just before crossing the bridge, swing left on Forest Road #122 leading to Holy Ghost Campground. There is a direction sign at this intersection. Follow the paved road 2.4 miles to a parking area located about 100 yards before the campground entrance. A sign opposite the parking area points to the trailhead.

HIKING INSTRUCTIONS: Leaving the parking area, the trail rises steeply, then proceeds up the canyon, bypassing the entire campground. Once past the campground, the trail crosses the stream on a foot bridge, and then follows Holy Ghost Creek upstream. After passing through some large meadows for about twenty minutes, you will cross Holy Ghost Creek from west to east. Another twenty minutes takes you to the second crossing and back to the west bank. In the meantime, you will have seen many wildflowers, and you will have been greatly tempted to linger among them. Next, you have a short steep climb up a ridge. You come to some aspen groves with beautiful fern; then you descend to the creek. After crossing it twice, you will be back on the west bank. You pass a grassy clearing surrounded by aspens, and soon afterwards cross the creek for the fifth time.

Once on the east bank, you turn away from the stream and begin the climb up the ridge between Holy Ghost Creek and Winsor Creek. During the next half hour, by a series of switchbacks, you will gain 650 feet in elevation. On the way up, you pass a small promontory, from which there is a fine view down into the Holy Ghost valley. You reach the top of a ridge and, at the northwest end of a meadow, the intersection with a trail (#254) coming up from Cowles. You are now three hours away from the starting point, and this is a good place to rest for a brief snack.

70

The walk continues in a northwesterly direction through a beautiful forest. In about thirty minutes you come to the intersection with another (shorter) trail (#261) from Cowles coming up on your right. Fifteen minutes later, you come to a point where you cross the main branch of Winsor Creek, which descends from Lake Katherine. After crossing the creek to its north bank, the trail splits in two. The Winsor Trail to Spirit Lake bears left, toward west. (The trail to the right goes north to Stewart Lake, less than half an hour away, and only one hundred feet above this junction. If you feel tired at this time, you may decide to go to Stewart Lake, instead of walking more than one hour and climbing seven hundred feet to Spirit Lake.)

After leaving the Winsor Creek crossing, the trail to Spirit Lake climbs fairly steeply, following Winsor Creek upstream. In several places, you get beautiful views of the stream as it cascades down its steep course. The trail becomes gradually easier as it passes some lush green meadows a short distance to the left. Twenty minutes after leaving the Winsor Creek crossing, you should begin to look for a trail junction, where the trail to Lake Katherine takes off to the right. This junction may have a signpost.

The Winsor Trail to Spirit Lake continues straight ahead. In five minutes, you will come to a somewhat confusing spot, where the trail crosses Winsor Creek from its north bank to the south bank. As you come closer to the creek, keep looking at the opposite bank for a blaze on a large spruce and for a low cairn. This marks the place where the Winsor Trail crosses to the south bank. Disregard the abandoned former Lake Katherine trail, which continues up the north side of Winsor Creek. Once across the creek, the trail is easy to follow as it climbs up the low ridge separating the Winsor and Holy Ghost drainages. You will reach the lake about half an hour after the last Winsor Creek crossing, and about five hours from the beginning of the walk.

The return trip will present no special problems. At the junctions with the trails from Cowles, remember to keep right. Shortly after the third crossing of Holy Ghost Creek on the return walk, as you walk parallel to the stream on its right (west) bank, you will come to a trail fork which you may not have noticed in the morning on the way up. Take the right branch, which goes up steeply for a short distance. On the home stretch through the streamside meadows, you may now feel that you have time for a more leisurely look at the many wildflowers.

(John Muchmore's helpful observations during joint walks over this route are gratefully acknowledged.)

72

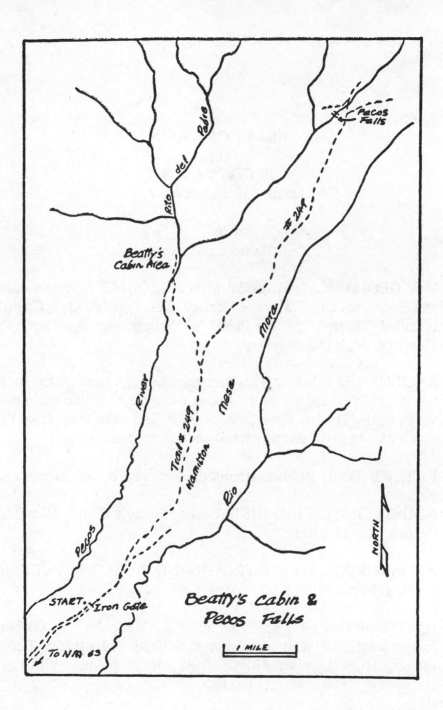

Rio del Pable

Pecos Falls

249

Beatty's Cabin Area

River

Mora

Trail # 249

Hamilton Mesa

Rio

Pecos

NORTH

START Iron Gate

To NM 63

Beatty's Cabin &
Pecos Falls

1 MILE

BEATTY'S CABIN
and
PECOS FALLS
(as an optional extension)

by
Philip L. Shultz

U.S. GEOLOGICAL SURVEY MAPS REQUIRED: Pecos Falls and Elk mountain - 7.5 minute series. Note that "Beatty's Cabin" is called "Beatty's" on the Pecos Wilderness map and "Beatty's Flats" on the USFS map.

SALIENT FEATURES: This hike goes through some of the most beautiful high meadows of the Pecos Wilderness, with outstanding views of the Truchas Peaks, Pecos Baldy and Lake Peak from the east side. In early summer the irises are spectacular.

RATING: Beatty's Cabin, strenuous; Pecos Falls, very strenuous.

ROUND TRIP HIKING DISTANCE: Beatty's Cabin, 10 miles; Pecos Falls, 17 miles.

APPROXIMATE ROUND TRIP HIKING TIME: Beatty's Cabin, 5 hours; Pecos Falls, 8 hours, stops not included.

ALTITUDE RANGE: Beatty's Cabin: Highest point, 10,200 feet; lowest point, 9400 feet; cumulative uphill hiking, 1640 feet. Pecos Falls: Highest point, 10,600 feet; lowest point, 9400 feet; cumulative uphill hiking, 1300 feet.

SEASONAL CONSIDERATIONS: This is not a winter hike. Four-wheel drive is required whenever the road is likely to be muddy.

ROUND TRIP DRIVING: 94 miles; approximately 3½ hours.

DRIVING DIRECTIONS: From Santa Fe take I-25 toward Las Vegas, New Mexico, for approximately 15 miles and exit on the Glorieta off-ramp #299. Turn left on the overpass, then turn right on State Road #50 and drive 6 miles to the town of Pecos. At the stop sign turn left onto State Road #63, which leads north into the Pecos River valley. Measure your mileage from this stop sign. From the Pecos stop sign, drive 18.5 miles, passing several camp and picnic grounds and the little settlement of Terrero. At the top of a grade turn right on Forest Road #223. A sign here will direct you to Iron Gate Campground. The distance between this junction and the campground is 4 miles; the road is steep and rough in places. Four-wheel drive is essential when the road is wet and muddy. (Remember the road may be dry in the morning but wet in the afternoon when you return after a summer shower.) Near the entrance of the campground you will find a parking area for hikers.

HIKING INSTRUCTIONS: The trail starts at the far end of the campground. Trail #249 gently zigzags northeast from the gate at the Iron Gate Campground. It rises about 300 feet in a little under half a mile, through spruce, fir and aspen to a usually well-marked junction with Trail #250 which goes essentially straight and makes up the right fork of the junction. Remain on Trail #249, bearing slightly left and still climbing. This is a popular trail for hikers and equestrians, so the trail marker signs may be torn down or defaced. In another quarter of a mile or so the trail comes out of the aspen, still climbing gently through the first meadow. In June the irises are gorgeous for the next 2 miles. Also, look for mariposa lilies. Kestrels are common and I have seen elk in these meadows on several occasions. The trail tops out at about 10,200 feet, a beautiful point for a rest stop, with fine views of the Truchas Peaks to the north. Three and a half miles from the start is the next marked trail junction, and the point of decision of whether to do the very long walk to Pecos Falls.

If you decide on the shorter trip to Beatty's Cabin, bear left (downhill to the northwest), entering the woods promptly for the winding descent to the Pecos River. Cross the good bridge and find a spot on the lovely grassy slope for a rest. The actual cabin is long gone. It was upstream near the confluence with the Rito del Padre. Return by the same route for a lovely, not too strenuous hike.

If you decide on the longer trip to Pecos Falls, instead of taking the left-hand trail to Beatty's Cabin, bear right on your original Trail #249. The trail generally follows the 10,200 foot contour through meadows and islands of aspen for about 4 miles to the falls, which are quite beautiful during the spring runoff when there is a good stream flowing. Return by retracing your walk along Trail #249 all the way back to Iron Gate Campground.

This wonderful high country is at its best in early summer when the irises are at their height, and in late September when the aspen leaves are golden. Enjoy it!

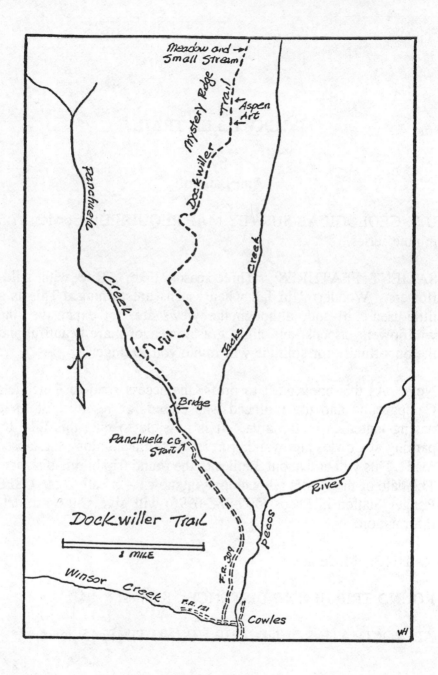

Meadow and
Small Stream

Aspen
Art

Mystery Ridge Trail

Dockwiller

Panchuela

Creek

Jacks

Creek

Fur

Bridge

Panchuela CG
Start

Dockwiller Trail

1 MILE

Pecos

River

Winsor   Creek

F.R. 309

F.R. 121

Cowles

WH

DOCKWILLER TRAIL

by
Ann Bancroft

U.S. GEOLOGICAL SURVEY MAP REQUIRED: Cowles - 7.5 minute series.

SALIENT FEATURES: Three-season hike. Rife with wild-flowers. Wonderful in fall when aspens are turning. This is a little-used trail and, although the views are not expansive, the wildflowers, aspens, and high, grassy meadows are beautiful and the opportunity for solitude will invite you to linger.

Note: As this book went to press, the access road to Panchuela Campground and the trailhead was closed for removal of toxic paving materials in the area. It is possible to take this hike by parking at Cowles and walking in to the trailhead along the closed road. This will add about 3 miles to the round trip hiking distance. The date of the road's reopening is unknown -- a call to the USFS Ranger Station in Pecos (505-988-6996) will give you up-to-date information.

RATING: Moderate.

ROUND TRIP HIKING DISTANCE: 8 miles.

APPROXIMATE ROUND TRIP HIKING TIME: 5 hours.

ALTITUDE RANGE: Highest point, 10,040 feet; lowest point, 8350 feet; cumulative uphill hiking, 1700 feet.

SEASONAL CONSIDERATIONS: Unhikeable in winter. Cool in summer because of dense aspen groves.

ROUND TRIP DRIVING: 91 miles; approximately 3 hours.

DRIVING DIRECTIONS: From Santa Fe take I-25 toward Las Vegas, New Mexico, for approximately 15 miles and exit on the Glorieta off-ramp #299. Turn left on the overpass, then turn right on State Road #50 and drive 6 miles to the town of Pecos. At the stop sign turn left onto State Road #63, which leads north into the Pecos River valley. Measure your mileage from this stop sign. From the Pecos stop sign, drive 20 miles to the road fork where the little settlement of Cowles used to be. Turn left, across the bridge onto Forest Road #121, and after just a few hundred yards turn sharply right uphill on Forest Road #305 toward Los Pinos Ranch and Panchuela Campground. (See Note, above.) The road dead-ends at Panchuela Campground in about 1.5 miles. Park on the right in the large open area reserved for hikers.

HIKING INSTRUCTIONS: From the parking area, walk a short distance upstream to a bridge which spans Panchuela Creek. Cross the bridge and continue hiking upstream along a well-defined trail. A gate will appear; be sure to close it after passing through. About 10 minutes of hiking will bring you to a sign which reads, "Horsethief Meadow 5½; Pecos Baldy Lake 8¼; Beatty's Cabin 9." Continue beyond the sign for another 10 minutes until the trail divides. Take the right fork uphill toward Pecos Baldy Lake and Beatty's Cabin. This steeply ascending switchbacked trail is the Dockwiller Trail, named after a man who lived in the Cowles area and ran a sawmill. It is also sometimes referred to as the Mystery Ridge Trail. What the mystery is I haven't been able to discover. The trail takes you uphill out of the Panchuela Creek drainage. In about 40 minutes you may spot the snow cornice between Santa Fe Baldy and Lake Peak toward the west.

After more severe switchbacks, at approximately 9200 feet, you will begin skirting the Jack's Creek drainage on the flank of Mystery Ridge. Continue along the trail which may sometimes become less well-defined as you pass through grassy areas. Off and on, aspen art may be spotted: the words "Dios nos libre, Amen" etched around a cross, or names, possibly of sheepherders, dating as far back as 1919.

After approximately 2½ hours, having taken a leisurely-paced hike with breaks, the turn-around point of this hike comes at a large sloping aspen-encircled meadow with a small stream running through it at approximately 10,000 feet. The trail continues on, but for this hike it's time to turn back, retracing your steps to Panchuela Campground.

(This hike leads to many other beautiful areas in the Pecos Wilderness. Someday you may want to go on to Beatty's Cabin or Horsethief Meadow or, if you have someone to do a drive-around, return to Jack's Creek Campground via the Round Mountain trail.)

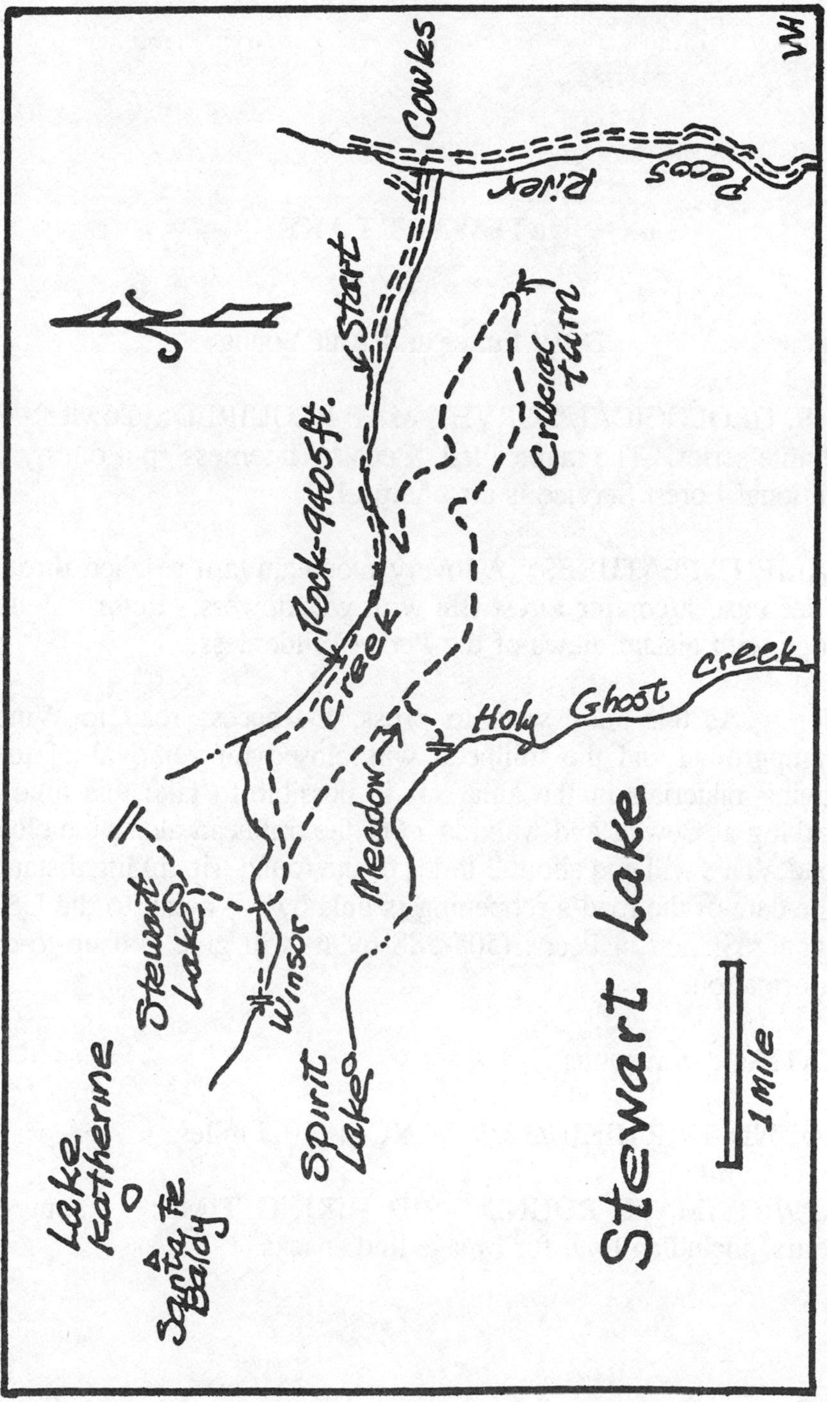

Stewart Lake

1 mile

Lake Katherine
Santa Fe Baldy

Spirit Lake

Stewart Lake

Winsor

Meadow

Holy Ghost creek

creek

Rock-9405 ft.

Start

Crucial turn

Cowles

Pecos River

NW

STEWART LAKE

by
Betsy Fuller and Ann Young

U.S. GEOLOGICAL SURVEY MAP REQUIRED: Cowles - 7.5 minute series. The map called "Pecos Wilderness" put out by the National Forest Service is also helpful.

SALIENT FEATURES: A lovely mountain tarn reached through a deep aspen/conifer forest rife with wildflowers. Return along a ridge with distant views of the Pecos Wilderness.

Note: As this book went to press, the access road to Winsor Campground and the trailhead was closed for removal of toxic paving materials in the area. It is possible to take this hike by parking at Cowles and walking in to the trailhead along the closed road. This will add about 2 miles to the round trip hiking distance. The date of the road's reopening is unknown -- a call to the USFS Ranger Station in Pecos (505-988-6996) will give you up-to-date information.

RATING: Strenuous.

ROUND TRIP HIKING DISTANCE: 10.5 miles.

APPROXIMATE ROUND TRIP HIKING TIME: About 6½ hours, including time for breaks and snacks.

ALTITUDE RANGE: Highest point, 10,332 feet; lowest point, 8400 feet; cumulative uphill hiking, 2500 feet.

SEASONAL CONSIDERATIONS: Beautiful in spring as soon as the snow disappears; good through fall until the first heavy snows.

ROUND TRIP DRIVING: 90 miles; 2 hours 45 minutes.

DRIVING DIRECTIONS: From Santa Fe take I-25 toward Las Vegas, New Mexico, for approximately 15 miles and exit on the Glorieta off-ramp #299. Turn left on the overpass, then turn right on State Road #50 and drive 6 miles to the town of Pecos. At the stop sign turn left onto State Road #63, which leads north into the Pecos River valley. Measure your mileage from this stop sign. From the stop sign, drive 20 miles to the junction where the little settlement of Cowles used to be. Turn left over the bridge onto Forest Road #121 and continue on for a little over a mile to the end of the road at Winsor Creek Campground. (See Note, above.)

HIKING INSTRUCTIONS: From the parking area, start hiking up the trail that parallels the creek. You'll walk through grassy meadows, aspen glades and wildflower patches. In 20 minutes or so you'll cross the stream to the left (south) bank and continue on the well-defined trail still paralleling the creek just below you.

(About one hundred yards after crossing the stream, you'll pass the trail that you will return on, but it is not marked in any way and is so obscure that you won't even notice it unless you know exactly where to look. Don't worry, it will be clear coming back.)

The aspens give way to deep conifer forests. You probably will notice a large rock sticking out partway into the trail with a U.S.G.S. marker imbedded in it indicating that the elevation is 9405 feet. This is a good place for a break since you will have been hiking for about an hour by now. Beyond this point the trail climbs higher and higher above the stream and finally you'll lose the sound of it below you. After about 15 more minutes of climbing beyond the rock, the trail levels out a little and another 15 minutes will bring you to a trail joining from the left. Note this junction well because on the return trip you will take the higher trail going back.

For now, though, continue on the trail ahead of you. In about 10 minutes of level walking you will cross a stream over a big log. This is the main fork of the Winsor Creek that you were paralleling down below. A sign here indicates the trail to Lake Katherine but for this hike continue straight ahead. Another 15 minutes will bring you to Stewart Lake. You'll have to climb up a little rise to get to it. There are many well-worn paths here, so take any one.

This little gem of a lake is spring fed and from its banks you can look up to the west and see the flanks of Santa Fe Baldy. Fishermen have worn a path around the lake, and after a snack and a rest you may want to walk around it. It won't take more than 15 or 20 minutes with time for admiring the wildflowers included.

To return, take the same path from the lake that you arrived on until you come to the trail junction mentioned previously. You can return the way you came, but a much more interesting way (although longer by about a mile and a half) is to take the right-hand trail that goes along the forested ridge above the trail you came on. (This trail does not show on the Cowles topo map, but if you have the map put out by the Forest Service called "Pecos Wilderness," you'll see it marked.)

In about 20 to 25 minutes from the junction you'll arrive at a meadow with a sign indicating that this is the Pecos Wilderness area. This sign may be vandalized, so if it isn't there or has been replaced by another sign don't worry. At this point -- the very beginning of the meadow -- your trail goes off to the left. It's quite faint here. Stay to the left of the meadow for a minute or two until the trail becomes more well defined. (If you find yourself crossing the meadow and dropping down into Holy Ghost Canyon to the right, you've missed your trail. Go back again to the top of the meadow and try again.) The trail is level or very slightly rising and in places where the grass is high becomes a little indistinct, but you should have no trouble finding it. It goes through aspen and then conifer forests and sometimes seems to be following an open swath through the trees. Was this once an ancient sheep-herding trail? You may see an occasional blaze on an old aspen. About 35 minutes after you've left the little meadow, an open view will begin to be visible in front of you. This is a nice spot for another break. Continue on the trail for another 20 minutes or so as the trail begins to descend.

Now you come to a place where you have to keep your eyes open because the trail takes a poorly marked sharp turn to the left. (This is about an hour from the trail junction and about 20 minutes from the place where the distant views become visible.) The landmarks to look for are a row of stones placed in a curve to the left, a few large branches to block passage straight ahead and, to your left, a large fallen ponderosa. Go past this ponderosa and the tall standing stump from which it broke and you'll quickly find the well defined trail going down the other side of the ridge you've been walking on. The trail turns back on itself toward the left. There may also be a small rock cairn here marking this important turn. (If you suddenly find yourself casting about for the trail you have probably gone a few yards too far. Back up a little and look for the landmarks mentioned above.)

From here on there are no problems. Look off to your right once in a while and you'll catch glimpses of Pecos Baldy, Round Mountain, Hamilton Mesa and Grass Mountain. The trail goes down, down, down, seemingly endlessly, and eventually, after about 45 minutes, you'll hear the stream down below you and then come to the trail on which you walked up to the lake. Another 20 minutes downstream will take you to your car.

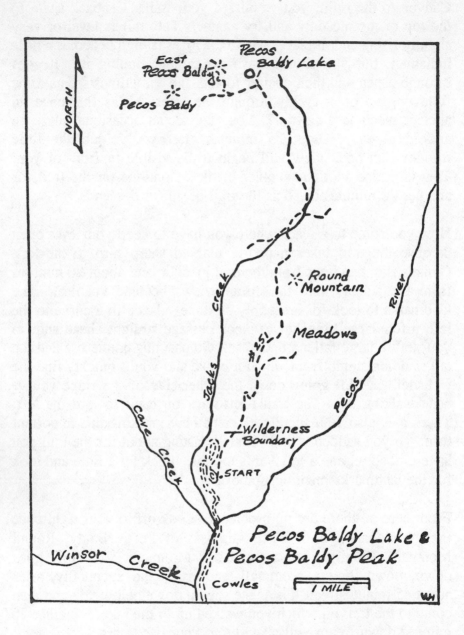

NORTH

Pecos Baldy Lake

East Pecos Baldy

Pecos Baldy

Round Mountain

Meadows

#251

Jacks Creek

Cave Creek

Pecos River

Wilderness Boundary

START

Winsor Creek

Cowles

Pecos Baldy Lake & Pecos Baldy Peak

1 MILE

WH

PECOS BALDY LAKE
and
PECOS BALDY PEAK

by
Betsy Fuller

U.S. GEOLOGICAL SURVEY MAPS REQUIRED: Cowles and Truchas Peak - 7.5 minute series.

SALIENT FEATURES: High country hike, magnificent vistas, wildflowers in summer, high grassy meadows, beautiful mountain lake with possibility of seeing bighorn sheep. Allow at least 11 hours round trip from Santa Fe. It's a long drive and a long hike, so get an early start. If your schedule allows, consider camping at Jack's Creek Campground the night before.

Note: As this book went to press, the access road to Jack's Creek Campground and the trailhead was closed for removal of toxic paving materials in the area. It is possible to take this hike by parking at Cowles and walking in to the trailhead along the closed road. This will add about 6 miles to the round trip hiking distance. The date of the road's reopening is unknown -- a call to the USFS Ranger Station in Pecos (505-988-6996) will give you up-to-date information.

RATING: Strenuous.

ROUND TRIP HIKING DISTANCE: 15 miles to Pecos Baldy Lake and 17 miles to East Pecos Baldy Peak.

87

APPROXIMATE ROUND TRIP HIKING TIME: 7½ hours to Pecos Baldy Lake and return; 9 hours to East Pecos Baldy Peak and return.

ALTITUDE RANGE: For Pecos Baldy Lake: Highest point, 11,320 feet; lowest point, 8850 feet; cumulative uphill hiking, 2600 feet. For East Pecos Baldy Peak: Highest point, 12,529 feet; lowest point, 8850 feet; cumulative uphill hiking, 3800 feet.

SEASONAL CONSIDERATIONS: A good summer and early fall walk. Probably impassable on foot after the first heavy snow in the fall. Spring flowers late June and July. Fall coloring September and early October. Higher sections of the trail can be muddy and boggy -- or even snow-packed -- in spring and early summer.

ROUND TRIP DRIVING: 102 miles; 3½ hours.

DRIVING DIRECTIONS: From Santa Fe take I-25 toward Las Vegas, New Mexico, for approximately 15 miles and exit on the Glorieta off-ramp #299. Turn left on the overpass, then turn right on State Road #50 and drive 6 miles to the town of Pecos. At the stop sign turn left onto State Road #63, which leads north into the Pecos River valley. Measure your mileage from this stop sign. From the Pecos stop sign drive 20 miles to the road fork where the little settlement of Cowles used to be. Do not take the road to the left which crosses the river, but keep straight ahead for another three miles following the Forest Service signs to Jack's Creek Campground. (See Note, above.) Keep to the right at every junction following the road to "Wilderness Parking" until you arrive at a large loop where there are picnic tables, a corral, and parking areas.

HIKING INSTRUCTIONS: The trailhead is to the north of the parking area where there is a Forest Service sign. The trail starts with a long climb (about a mile) through a conifer forest up the side of a hill. During this climb you will enter the Pecos Wilderness. Soon after the initial long climb, the trail goes into a series of long switchbacks still rising, until finally, after about another mile, the trail levels off a little. Just after another short climb, you will reach an open sloping grassy area. At this point, there is a signpost marking a "Y" trail junction. You will have walked about 2.5 miles and climbed about 1050 feet. Your altitude here is 10,026 feet.

Take the left (north) fork of the trail and continue through the meadow toward the aspen trees. After passing through the aspens, the trail swings slightly to the right. Watch for beautiful distant views of the Pecos Valley to the east and the mountains to the west as you look all around you. The trail climbs up through an open meadow in a northerly direction. Soon you will get your first view of the barren Pecos Baldy Peaks looming above the forests to the northwest. At the northern end of this meadow the trail enters a conifer forest and drops down to Jack's Creek, which is shallow most of the year and can easily be crossed on stepping stones. At this point you will have walked another 2 miles in about 45 minutes to an hour.

Crossing Jack's Creek, follow the trail to the right paralleling the stream. In 5 minutes, the trail swings away from the stream. Fifteen minutes after crossing Jack's Creek, the trail splits. Go straight ahead to Pecos Baldy, not right to Beatty's Cabin. Continue climbing through deep and dark conifer forests. Your altitude here is now over 10,500 feet and the trail is steep in some places, so take it easy as you continue your ascent.

Finally, about 2 miles (and over an hour's walking) after you crossed Jack's Creek, you will leave the forest behind you and will see the summit of East Pecos Baldy Peak ahead of you. One last steep climb brings you out at yet another junction from which point you will see Pecos Baldy Lake just a few hundred feet away. As you approach the lake, note the ridgeline of East Pecos Baldy Peak sloping downward to your left and ending at a high open saddle. This is the open saddle you cross on the way up to the peak.

If you're tired (and you will be!) go down to the lake for a snack and a rest. As you're recovering from the steep walk, search the sides of the mountain for bighorn sheep which are often found here in the summer months. Sometimes the sheep are overly friendly, nuzzling into your knapsack if it's left unattended. It will make a great picture, though, if you have a camera handy.

You may want to end the outward bound trip here. If you've still got enough energy left, you might want to consider two options: climb East Pecos Baldy Peak or climb the ridge north of the lake.

Option #1: To climb East Pecos Baldy (2 miles round trip, 1100 feet up), go back up a couple of hundred feet to the place where you first saw the lake and where there is a marker prohibiting camping in the lake basin. Take the trail to the southwest (to your right as you walk away from the lake) and follow it for about one-half mile through a forested hillside south of the lake until it comes out into an open saddle. Don't take the trail to the left that goes downhill through the woods, but continue across the open saddle in the same general direction that you were following when you arrived. You will have no trouble finding the rocky path that now zigzags up the steep side of the mountain. The climb from the saddle to the top of East Pecos Baldy is another 680 feet and a hard pull at this elevation (12,529 feet when you reach the top), so take your time and enjoy the ever enlarging views as you climb to the top. Don't attempt this part of the hike if it's stormy. There's no protection on top, and lightning and strong winds are not good companions when you're on the top of a bare rocky peak in the high mountains. There is frequently a snow cornice along the peak, with a considerable overhang. Do not walk out on any snow field along the edge of the peak.

Option #2: Go up to the saddle of the ridge north of the lake (1 mile round trip, 400 feet up). Keeping the lake on your left, walk to the north side of the lake and then up to the saddle. There are several trails leading in the same direction. Your reward will be terrific views of the mountains to the north. And yes, those are fossils in the gray shale outcrops. Go back to the lake the same way you came up.

Your return trip is over the same route as the one you came up on, the only difference (an important one!) being that you'll be going downhill most of the time.

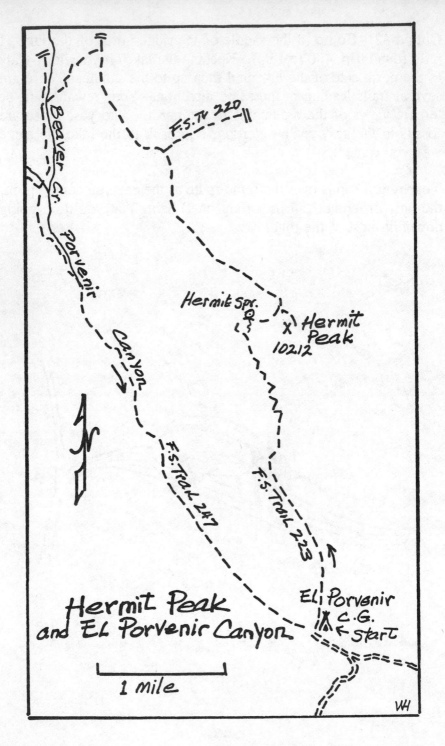

Hermit Peak
and El Porvenir Canyon

1 mile

Beaver Cr.

Porvenir

Canyon

F.S. Tk 220

Hermit Spr.

X Hermit Peak
10212

F.S. Trail 247

F.S. Trail 223

El Porvenir
C.G.
← Start

N

VH

HERMIT PEAK
and
EL PORVENIR CANYON
(as an optional extension)

by
Norbert Sperlich

U.S. GEOLOGICAL SURVEY MAPS REQUIRED: El Porvenir, and, for the extended hike, Rociada - 7.5 minute series. On top of Hermit Peak, a section of Trail #223 (from Hermit Spring to the east rim) has been rerouted; this new route does not appear on the topo map.

SALIENT FEATURES: Hermit Peak is a rugged granite peak and major landmark in the southeastern corner of the Pecos Wilderness. It is named for a hermit who lived in a cave near the summit in the 1860s. The approach to the trailhead is on paved roads. The trail is quite steep. From the summit are great views toward the eastern plains.

The extension of this hike takes you into beautiful El Porvenir Canyon with its meadows, wildflowers, waterfalls, and rugged cliffs. You will be challenged by 25 or more stream crossings, and an extra pair of sneakers and socks, a walking stick, and mosquito repellent might be helpful for this adventure. Don't attempt the canyon during spring runoff! It is a long hike and a long drive, so start early. To get an early start, you might want to spend the night at El Porvenir Campground.

RATING: Hermit Peak, moderate in distance, but strenuous if you are not used to steep climbs. Hermit Peak and El Porvenir Canyon, strenuous.

ROUND TRIP HIKING DISTANCE: Hermit Peak, 8 miles. Hermit Peak and El Porvenir Canyon, about 14 miles.

APPROXIMATE ROUND TRIP HIKING TIME: Hermit Peak, 5 hours. Hermit Peak and El Porvenir Canyon, about 7 hours, stops not included.

ALTITUDE RANGE: Highest point, 10,212 feet; lowest point, 7550 feet; cumulative uphill hiking, approximately 2700 feet for Hermit Peak, about 2800 feet for Hermit Peak and El Porvenir Canyon.

SEASONAL CONSIDERATIONS: Not a winter hike. For the El Porvenir Canyon portion of the hike, avoid the spring runoff.

ROUND TRIP DRIVING: 170 miles; approximately 3½ hours.

DRIVING DIRECTIONS: Take I-25 toward Las Vegas, New Mexico. Take the first exit into Las Vegas and turn left onto road #329. There is a sign, "United World College," at the turnoff. Turn left again at a stop light where road #329 crosses Hot Spring Road. You are now on road #65, which will take you to the trailhead. After passing United World College (on the right) in Montezuma, the road starts to climb and becomes narrow, with many blind curves. When you approach the village of Gallinas, the rocky face of Hermit Peak appears in the background. Look for green mileage markers on the right side of the road. After mile 13, you will come to a fork. Take the right branch to El Porvenir. After about 2.7 miles, you will reach the parking lot at the entrance to El Porvenir Campground. Park here. A sign, "Hermit Peak Trail Head," points to a wooden bridge.

HIKING INSTRUCTIONS: Cross the wooden bridge next to the parking lot. After a few minutes, you will be back on the road that leads to the campground. Look for a trailhead marked, "Hermit Peak, Trail #223," just before the road comes to the campers' self-service pay station. The trail starts to climb right away. After a few minutes, it goes through a fence. Shortly after, the Dispensas Trail branches off to the right. Keep on going straight, following the sign, "Hermit Peak 4." The trail crosses two drainages. Next, two old roads merge with the trail, coming in from the right. Some 40 yards past the place where your trail joins the second road, this road turns left, crossing a low spot where two drainages come in from the right. Here, your trail leaves the road and goes off to the right at a 90 degree angle, and up a ridge between the two drainages that come in from the right. This junction is usually marked; however, in August 1994 the sign was missing.

From now on, the trail is wide and obvious, and there are no more forks until you reach the summit plateau. You can forget about the trail for a while and enjoy your surroundings. As you go up and up, ponderosa pines give way to Douglas firs and aspen. The slope gets steeper and the trail starts to zigzag up a canyon formed by the cliffs of Hermit Peak. An intermittent stream runs through this canyon, and you might notice a sign, "Trail Spring," which points to the stream. After about 2 hours of hiking, you will come to the top of the cliffs. Enjoy the view.

The trail now moves away from the rim. In a minute or two, you might notice an old trail going up to the right. Ignore it. Soon, you will reach a clearing. Here is Hermit Spring, enclosed in rock walls and protected with a metal cover. Hermit Peak (actually the east rim) is only one-half mile away, and you have a choice of two trails to get there. The new, official route, passing to the left of the spring, is indicated by a trail sign. The old trail, no longer marked, turns right in front of the spring. It is lined with wooden crosses. Only the new trail has a marked junction where you can go in the direction of Lone Pine Mesa and eventually into El

Porvenir Canyon. So, if you plan to do the extended hike, use the new trail, as described here.

After about 10 more minutes of hiking, you will come to a fork in the trail. Trail #223, the trail you have been on, turns sharply to the left and goes to Lone Pine Mesa. You go straight ahead on Trail #223A, toward the peak, as indicated on the signpost. Soon the rim of the summit plateau will appear on your left. In 5 minutes, you will be at the edge of Hermit Peak, looking across the plains to the east.

There are several old trails on the summit plateau. Make sure you return the way you came, with the mountain's edge close to your right. After about 5 minutes, you will come to the marked trail fork again. The left fork will take you back the same way you came up. If you are planning to take the long way back by way of El Porvenir Canyon, you should now take the right branch, toward Lone Pine Mesa. You have 10 more miles ahead of you! Do you have enough time?

The trail to El Porvenir Canyon will take you through a conifer and aspen forest, heading in a northwesterly direction. Soon it starts to drop down, staying on a ridge all the time. After some ups and downs, the trail levels out. About two miles from Hermit Peak, you will come to a trail junction marked by signposts and a cairn. Your trail (#223) goes left toward Lone Pine Mesa. Trail #220 (Rito Chavez Trail) goes straight ahead (Trail #220 does not appear on the 1965 topo map). The trail is little-used and faint in places. It goes down, then up again, following a ridge which becomes narrow and rocky. About 1.2 miles or 25 minutes after the last trail junction, you will come to another fork marked by signposts and cairns (the sign boards were gone in 1993). Take the trail that goes down to the left, towards Beaver Creek Canyon. On your way down, you will get glimpses of the canyon, and after about 25 minutes of steep downhill hiking you will reach Beaver Creek and a "T" junction marked by a cairn and a signpost. A marker, "Lone

Pine Mesa, Hermit Peak," points in the direction you have come from. This is a great place for a stop. Right across from the trail, Beaver Creek forms a waterfall and a pool.

To continue the hike, take the left branch of the "T" junction, following Beaver Creek downstream. From now on, you will hike along lively streams, first Beaver Creek, then Porvenir Creek. This is the wild and wonderful part of the hike, 5 miles of hiking through meadows and woods, alongside rushing water and towering cliffs. If you brought extra sneakers for the stream crossings, now is the time to put them on.

After crossing Beaver Creek 4 times, you will reach a marked trail junction where the trail you are on (Trail #247) meets Trail #219 (Hollinger Creek Trail), the latter coming in from the right. Keep on going downstream on Trail #247.

You are now in Porvenir Canyon. Soon the canyon narrows, with the granite cliffs of Hermit Peak on one side and El Cielo Mountain on the other. And yes, there are stream crossings galore. Stick to the trail and do not try to skip a crossing by staying on "this side." It does not work. The last two miles of the hike are on private land; stay on the trail to avoid trespassing. When the canyon widens again, you are coming to the end of the hike. You will pass campsites and the remains of a log cabin, and reach a sign directing you to the Parking Area. Go through a gate and soon you will arrive at the parking lot where you left your car. By now, you will be bouncing along in exhilaration, looking for more stream crossings, or you may be staggering on wobbly legs. It is up to you!

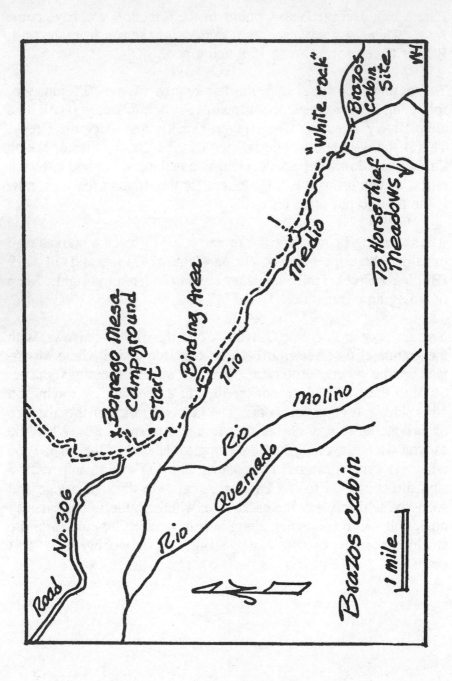

BRAZOS CABIN

by
John O. Baxter

U.S. GEOLOGICAL SURVEY MAPS REQUIRED: Sierra Mosca and Truchas Peak - 7.5 minute series. (The trail shown on these maps is different from the current trail described here.)

SALIENT FEATURES: This trail into the Pecos Wilderness is used less than trails starting at the Santa Fe Ski Basin. A beautiful mountain country hike, mostly in the trees, with good bird and flower sightings likely. The destination of this hike is a high meadow with views of Pecos Baldy.

The Forest Service access road #306 was in good condition in 1994 (a dry year). After prolonged rains, you should check with the Forest Service about road conditions.

RATING: Strenuous.

ROUND TRIP HIKING DISTANCE: 11 miles.

APPROXIMATE ROUND TRIP HIKING TIME: 7 hours.

ALTITUDE RANGE: Highest point, 9200 feet; lowest point, 8250 feet; cumulative uphill hiking, 1550 feet. There is a sharp drop (8850 to 8250 feet) in the first half mile, then a gradual climb to Brazos Cabin at 9200 feet.

SEASONAL CONSIDERATIONS: May be snowed-in in winter.

ROUND TRIP DRIVING: 78 miles; approximately 2½ hours.

DRIVING DIRECTIONS: Take US #84/285 northbound to Pojoaque (about 16 miles from Santa Fe) and turn right onto NM #503 at the Nambé turnoff (traffic light). Note the mileage at the turnoff. At the Cundiyo-Chimayo junction, go straight ahead toward Cundiyo. Drive carefully through Cundiyo (narrow road, free-roaming dogs). About two miles past Cundiyo, you will pass a turnoff to Santa Cruz Lake on your left. Just past this turnoff, look for Forest Road #306, which goes off to the right. This turnoff is 13.5 miles from the Nambé turnoff, where you took your odometer reading. Turn right onto FR #306 and follow it for 9 miles to a junction with FR #435. Before you reach this junction, you will pass a turnoff on your right marked Trail #150, Borrego Trail. This is not your trail. Close to the Borrego Mesa Campground, FR #306 curves to the left. Here, you turn right onto FR #435, which takes you to the entrance of the campground. Now take the road that goes off to the right in front of the entrance. It is about 300 yards to the trailhead of Trail #155. The last part of this road was very rutted in September 1994. You might want to park closer to the entrance of the campground, especially if rain is expected.

HIKING INSTRUCTIONS: At the trailhead, to the right of the road, you will find an information board with a trail description. A wooden sign directs you to Rio Medio Trail #155, which reaches the junction with the Rio Capulin Trail after 5 miles and Trail Riders Wall after 10 miles. You will follow this trail to Brazos Cabin for about 5.5 miles. The trail sets off in an easterly direction, rising slightly for 100 yards before plunging sharply down into Rio Medio Canyon. Much of this trail was rerouted in 1992. If you find yourself on a washed-out, rutted trail, you have probably strayed from the new, narrow trail onto the old one. This is most likely to happen on the stretch between the trailhead and the place where the trail reaches the river for the first time. Retrace your steps and get back on the new trail.

On the right, the green silhouette of Sierra Mosca looms over the valley to the south. Winding through towering ponderosas and patches of oak, the trail makes a descent of 600 feet in the first half mile, leading to the clear waters of the Rio Medio. Don't forget that this same steep slope must be negotiated in reverse at the end of the hike when the scenery may seem less remarkable.

Continuing eastward, the track follows the north bank of the river upstream. Birders should find several mountain species in this area such as Steller's jays, hairy woodpeckers and western wood peewees. Broadtailed hummingbirds are often seen feeding at the scarlet penstemon blossoms which border the trail. Unfortunately, the canyon is also the home of some of New Mexico's most belligerent insects, including clouds of voracious gnats in June and equally hungry deer flies later on. THAT'S why they call it Sierra Mosca (Fly Mountain)!

After staying close to the Rio Medio for about a mile, the trail leaves the bottom of the canyon to climb up on the north bank for the next 2.5 miles or so, making several swings away from the river to cross a series of arroyos which come down from the north. If a snack now seems in order, reward yourself with the tiny raspberries which grow in profusion nearby as the trail returns to the Medio. At this point a large boulder protrudes over the rushing stream, which older hikers will instantly recognize as the perch of the White Rock nymph, one of the classic advertising symbols of an earlier era. Chances of seeing the maiden herself are less certain.

Because the canyon is much narrower here, the trail is forced close to the creek and it is necessary to clamber along the face of sheer granite cliffs in a few places. After making an easy crossing on a huge ponderosa, the trail passes through a log fence into a horse corral and comes to a marked fork. Here, Trail #158 goes off to the right toward Horse Thief Meadow. Stay on Trail #155 (the left fork). It takes you out of the corral, through a most picturesque section of the canyon, and in a few short minutes reaches a beautiful meadow where Brazos Cabin once stood. Of the cabin, only some foundation stones remain. In this part of the valley, which opens rather suddenly, there are many pleasant locations to enjoy your lunch and the beauty of the Sangre de Cristos before retracing your footsteps towards the trailhead.

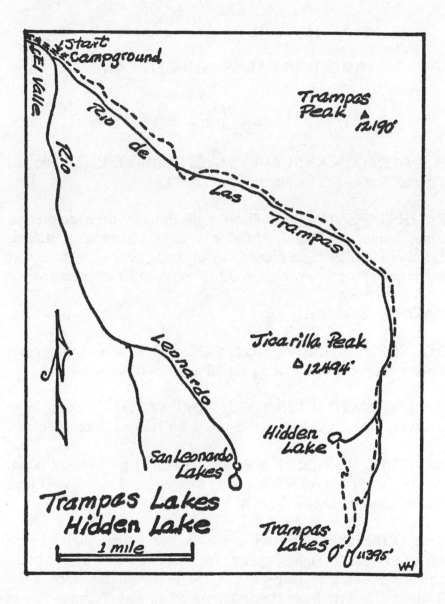

Start
Campground

El Valle

Rio de Las Trampas

Rio

Trampas Peak △ 12190'

Jicarilla Peak △ 12494'

Leonardo

San Leonardo Lakes

Hidden Lake

Trampas Lakes ○ △ 11395'

N

Trampas Lakes
Hidden Lake

1 mile

VH

TRAMPAS LAKES - HIDDEN LAKE

by
Betsy Fuller

U.S. GEOLOGICAL SURVEY MAPS REQUIRED: El Valle and Truchas Peak - 7.5 minute series.

SALIENT FEATURES: Good trail through deep coniferous forests, much of the time above a clear fast-running stream. Lovely hidden lakes surrounded by towering peaks. Wildflowers in season. Progresses through 3 life zones and a riparian zone.

RATING: Strenuous.

ROUND TRIP HIKING DISTANCE: 11.5 miles to Trampas Lakes; extension to Hidden Lake, 2 additional miles.

APPROXIMATE ROUND TRIP HIKING TIME: 6 hours to Trampas Lakes. Additional 1½ hours for Hidden Lake extension.

ALTITUDE RANGE: Highest point, 11,410 feet; lowest point, 9000 feet; cumulative uphill hiking to Trampas Lakes, 2450 feet, and to Hidden Lake, 2700 feet.

SEASONAL CONSIDERATIONS: A late spring, summer, and early fall walk. (Cautionary Note: Winter cross-country and back-country skiers who may be tempted to ski in the Rio de las Trampas Canyon from the campground to Las Trampas Lakes should be fully aware of the avalanche danger. This danger becomes greater toward spring and on warm winter days with widely-changing temperatures. Travelling the Rio de las Trampas Canyon trail during such conditions is to be avoided.)

ROUND TRIP DRIVING: About 108 miles; 3 hours.

DRIVING DIRECTIONS: Take US #84/285 north for about 17 miles from the plaza, past the turn-off to Los Alamos (State Road #502), and continue on #84/285 another 0.5/mile to the stoplight at the junction with State Road #503. Turn right (east) on SR #503 toward Chimayo. About 7.5 miles from the turn-off onto SR #503, take a left turn (north) onto State Road #520 to Chimayo. Go through the little settlement of Chimayo until you come to the junction with State Road #76. Turn right (east) on SR #76 toward Truchas. About 7.7 miles from this junction and just as you get into the settled part of the village of Truchas, #76 takes a sharp turn to the left (north). The turn here is between two buildings and hardly looks like a main thoroughfare but there is a sign here showing that the road goes to Peñasco and Picuris. It may also be identified as the High Road to Taos.

Take a new odometer reading and continue on #76 through the villages of Ojo Sarco and Las Trampas (Spanish for "traps"). Soon after you pass through the village of Las Trampas, be sure to notice the old log flume on the right, still carrying water from the higher elevations over the ravine to the irrigation ditches of the village below. About 8.7 miles past Truchas and about a mile beyond Trampas, you come to Forest Service Road #207 (sometimes unmarked) going off to the right (east). Take this road and drive past the settlement of El Valle. From El Valle to the very end of FS #207 is about 8.1 miles. The road ends at a primitive campground. Park here.

HIKING INSTRUCTIONS: Now you can get a close look at the Rio de las Trampas whose course you have been following in the car. It comes rushing out of a deep little canyon, probably the reason the road comes to an end here.

Forest Trail #31 starts up about 20 feet on the hill to your left as you face up the river. After this initial clamber, the trail starts its steady upward path. You are at about 8960 feet here and you have about 2400 feet to climb to the lakes, and over 5 miles. You will pass through a gate (be sure to close it behind you) and after about 45 minutes the trail will cross to the south side of the stream and then again to the north side. This is where a snow avalanche came down the side of the mountain a few years ago taking all the trees down with it (see <u>Cautionary Note</u>, above). The area is now regenerating into an aspen forest usually filled with a profusion of wildflowers.

Until you get very near the lakes, you will be walking along the left side of the river, most of the time quite far above it, but within earshot of it and with occasional glimpses of it rushing below you. There are many long switchbacks that help ease your way up, and, finally, several crossings of the river which, except during the spring snow melt, should be no problem. Fallen tree trunks and stepping stones can be useful in crossing.

At the right time of year, usually early to mid-July, you find unbelievably beautiful gardens of marsh marigolds, brook cress, false hellebore, wild candytuft, thimbleberry, cranesbill, osha, cow parsnip, Parry's primrose and many, many other flowers. Look back down the valley once in a while and you will catch glimpses of the flat land around Española below you in the Rio Grande valley. The views are not expansive, but you will get a good idea of how high up you are.

Finally you will top out at a level, sometimes marshy, area. Although you cannot see the lakes from here, there should be a sign identifying them, and a walk of a few hundred yards straight ahead will bring you to them. They are separated from each other by a low ridge and both provide beautiful sites for lunch and photographs.

EXTENSION: From these lakes you can either return directly to your car down the trail over which you have just come or you can take an extension to Hidden Lake. This extension will consume about 1½ hours including time for a snack at the lake and will add about 2 miles to the total distance.

If you want to go on to Hidden Lake, return to the place where you topped out, and where the sign identifying Trampas Lakes is. Then, instead of going back down the steep trail you came up, bear to your left. You will be walking along a good trail that is almost parallel with the trail you came on, but above it. Gradually the trail to Hidden Lake will bear off to the left, and, after a couple of mild switchbacks, you will descend to the lake itself. You will have dropped about 280 feet from the Trampas Lakes to Hidden Lake, and you will now have to climb back up in order to start the return trek home.

The return trip to your car is over the same trail on which you walked to get to the lakes. Tighten your boot laces because it's downhill all the way!

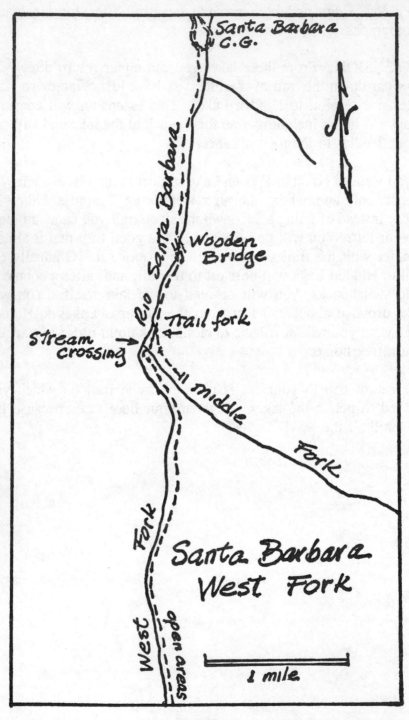

Santa Barbara C.G.

Rio Santa Barbara

Wooden Bridge

Trail fork

Stream Crossing

Middle Fork

Santa Barbara West Fork

West Fork

open areas

1 mile

SANTA BARBARA WEST FORK

by
Linda and John Buchser

U.S. GEOLOGICAL SURVEY MAP REQUIRED: Jicarita Peak
- 7.5 minute series.

SALIENT FEATURES: This trip takes you to the north end of the
Pecos Wilderness. Following the West Fork of Santa Barbara
Creek, you will hike through lush meadows and aspen forest to
alpine tundra, depending on the distance you travel.

RATING: Easy to strenuous.

ROUND TRIP HIKING DISTANCE: 6 to 12 miles.

APPROXIMATE ROUND TRIP HIKING TIME: 3½-7 hours.

ALTITUDE RANGE: Highest point, 9880 feet; lowest point, 8868
feet; cumulative uphill hiking, 1100 feet.

SEASONAL CONSIDERATIONS: Road closed several miles
before Santa Barbara campground during snow season.

ROUND TRIP DRIVING: 143 miles; 2½-3 hours.

DRIVING DIRECTIONS: From Santa Fe take US #84/285 north
to Española. In Española, stay on the main road as US #84/285
goes off to the left. Continuing straight ahead, you will be on New

Mexico #68 headed toward Taos. Go through Velarde and along the Rio Grande to Embudo, where you turn right (east) onto New Mexico #75. Continue through Dixon and Peñasco. When you come toward the end of Peñasco, Highway #75 turns sharply left (toward Vadito). Don't take this left turn. Keep on going straight ahead toward Rodarte. After about 1.5 miles, the road you are on will turn right. Just before you come to this turn, look for a dirt road that goes off to the left. This is your road, Forest Service Road #116. There might be a brown Forest Service sign directing you to Santa Barbara campground. Follow this dirt road for six miles to Santa Barbara campground.

HIKING INSTRUCTIONS: Park in the area before the cattle guard entrance to the campground, and hike above the campground on the trail.

Beginning at the southern end of Santa Barbara campground, the foot trail passes through a fence and crosses a small feeder stream prior to joining the main horse trail. At about one mile, the trail is rerouted to avoid a washed-out area and ascends through an aspen stand. Looking down from this higher portion, one can see a beaver lodge and a dam on a side area of the creek. Later, the trail runs along the main flow of Santa Barbara Creek.

In a normally wet year there is a continuous show of wildflowers from April through September, and a great variety, since the changes in habitat and elevation provide a wide range of growing conditions. At about 1.6 miles, there is a wooden bridge crossing the creek. This first section of trail, and the return, is an easy day hike for those with small children or small energies. Now the trail increases its rate of ascent. At about 2.3 miles you will come to a trail fork marked by a sign. The left fork, which you do not take, is Middle Fork Trail #24. Go straight ahead on West Fork Trail #25. In another 0.2/mile there is a stream crossing which often has a number of peeled logs jammed across as a makeshift bridge.

* (If it is the rainy season, you may find these logs dry enough to cross on the way in, but under water on the way out. In this case, the creek may be forded just upstream of the logs, but use caution in the swift water and expect to get wet up to your hips. During the spring runoff, the stream may be too deep to ford at all.)

The stream you have just crossed is actually a combination of the East and Middle Forks and you are now between them and the West Fork, which is out of sight at this point. The trail moves higher on the mountainside, and though the West Fork is now often visible, access to it is down inconveniently steep and loose slopes.

At about mile 4.7, you come out of the trees and pass through open areas. On the stream below are more beaver dams. These intermittent meadows continue to the end of the valley. Cattle grazing is permitted here only in the fall of every third year, so meadow wildflowers can be magnificent when there has been sufficient rain. Chimayosos Mountain comes into view spectacularly to the south.

(Approximately 5 miles in, you will pass on the right a sign for the Dominguez Trail, which connects the West Fork drainage with the Trampas River drainage. This re-routing of an old sheepherders' trail was the product of several years' worth of national Sierra Club trail maintenance service trips.)

You reach the end of the meadows at about mile 6, with a sign indicating another 6 miles to the divide. The trail goes on up to the Santa Barbara Divide, but this is the turn-around point for this hike.

Return by the same route.

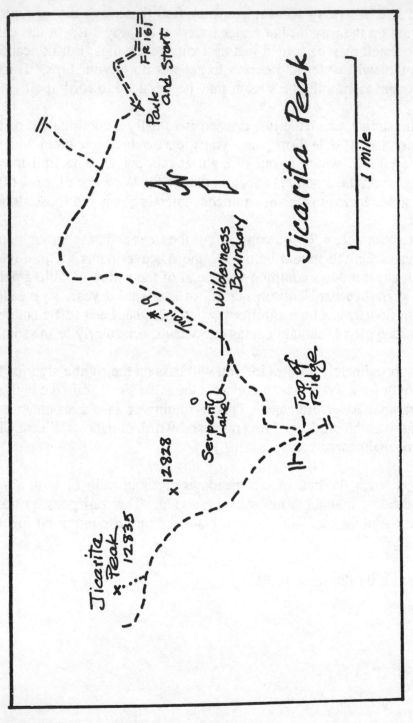

Jicarita Peak

1 mile

FR 161
Park and Start

Trail 19

Wilderness Boundary

Serpent Lake

Top of Ridge

x 12828

Jicarita Peak
x 12835

JICARITA PEAK

by
Norma McCallan

U.S. GEOLOGICAL SURVEY MAP REQUIRED: Jicarita Peak - 7.5 minute series shows this area, but it neither shows Forest Road #161 nor is an accurate portrayal of the current trail. Use the USFS Pecos Wilderness map.

SALIENT FEATURES: This hike to the tenth highest peak in New Mexico affords marvelous vistas of the surrounding countryside, incredible displays of alpine wildflowers, and a sense of being on the very top of the world. The peak itself is easily climbed, and can be done as a day hike. Because the peak and its approach are well above timberline, caution is urged in the event of approaching storms. Frequent thunderstorms play around the Santa Barbara Divide in the summer, and that exposed terrain is not the place to be when lightning is striking.

RATING: Strenuous.

ROUND TRIP HIKING DISTANCE: Approximately 11 miles.

APPROXIMATE ROUND TRIP HIKING TIME: 6-9 hours.

ALTITUDE RANGE: Highest point, 12,835 feet; lowest point, 10,400; cumulative uphill hiking, 2435 feet.

SEASONAL CONSIDERATIONS: June to October would be best; earlier or later one may run into snow, and even June or October could be risky. The dirt road to the trailhead is not plowed in the winter.

ROUND TRIP DRIVING: 151 miles; 4 hours.

DRIVING DIRECTIONS: Take US #84/285 north out of Santa Fe for approximately 17 miles from the plaza past the turn-off to Los Alamos (State Road #502) and continue on for about 0.5/mile to the stoplight at the junction with State Road #503. Turn right (east) on State Road #503 toward Chimayo. About 7.5 miles from the turn-off onto State Road #503, take a left turn (north) onto State Road #520 to Chimayo. Go through the settlement of Chimayo until you come to the junction with State Road #76. Turn right (east) on State Road #76 toward Truchas. About 7.7 miles from the turn and just as you get into the settled part of the village of Truchas, #76 takes a sharp turn to the left (north). The turn here is between two buildings and hardly looks like a main thoroughfare, but there is a prominent sign here showing that the road goes to Chamisal and Peñasco. Continue on #76 through the villages of Ojo Sarco, Las Trampas, and Chamisal. Turn right onto state Road #75 just before the village of Peñasco and continue through Peñasco. At the end of Peñasco, turn left, still on #75, through Vadito. When, ten minutes from Peñasco, you come to a "T" intersection, turn right onto State Road #518. This road goes past a number of Forest Service campgrounds and through the small village of Tres Ritos. At 1.7 miles past the sign to the private Angostura Camp and at 0.9/mile past the sign for Mora County, turn right onto Forest Service Road #161. It is marked with a large brown sign on the highway. Stay on this rough but passable road until it dead ends after 4.6 miles, and park.

HIKING INSTRUCTIONS: At the trailhead, you will see a large brown Forest Service marker identifying the trail ahead as Trail #19. Ignore the trail to the right which is identified as Angostura

Trail #18 and Angostura Campground. Proceed on Trail #19, which is really an extension of the road you have been driving on. Within a quarter mile or so you will see another Forest Service sign saying Serpent Lake Trail 3 miles and Santa Barbara Campground, both to the left. Follow the left hand trail. Shortly thereafter you will see a small unmarked trail to the right, and then a wider, also unmarked, trail to the right. Ignore both. Note this second intersection so that on your return you do not follow a blue arrow in a tree pointing left. (The arrow is not visible as you are going up the trail.) Very shortly you will cross a fast-flowing ditch; there should be enough stones and logs to make a relatively easy crossing.

The trail continues through the forest, going upward at a comfortable incline. About 1.5 miles in you will pass a series of meadows, which make a good spot for a rest stop since this part of the trail is mostly heavy forest. Slightly more than 2.5 miles in, you will come to a boundary sign for the Pecos Wilderness. Soon thereafter, as you turn a corner, you will see the stark outline of the Santa Barbara Divide through the trees. Less than a half mile further you will come to the intersection of the Serpent Lake Trail, heading off to the right, while the main trail has a sign showing that it is 11 miles further to Santa Barbara Campground and 10 miles back to Agua Piedra Campground. Serpent Lake is only about a quarter mile down the side trail.

Continue up the main trail. It soon leaves the forest and starts to switchback up through the scree and isolated clumps of stunted spruce and bristlecone pine. As you go higher, these pygmy forests give way to dense patches of willow, and magnificent bouquets of alpine flowers dot the scree. By September, most the flowers have died off, but the willows are turning gold and so are the aspen in the surrounding forests. Just before you get to the top of the Divide you will pass a small spring, which takes the form of a shallow pond, on the right.

Once on top you will find an old sign pointing back down the trail with the barely legible legend that Serpent Lake is 2 miles and Agua Piedra Campground is also that way. About 50 feet further stands a post where a sign used to be, showing the Santa Barbara Campground to be 9 miles away. Do not continue any further on this Angostura Trail, which meanders over the ridge and switchbacks down to the Middle Fork of the Santa Barbara River, even though it will have the more prominent cairns and better worn path. Instead, while standing by this post, look to your right, and you should see one large cairn, and perhaps patches of trail heading northwest. Walk there. Once at this first cairn, look in the same direction you have just walked and you should see a second cairn, and then a third. Follow these cairns as the trail contours along the ridge near the top of the Divide and detours around the south side of a large unnamed 12,828 foot peak. In some stretches, alternate trails and cairns exist -- don't worry, they all seem to end up in the same place.

Not until you are well around this peak will Jicarita Peak itself be visible -- its flat top and trapezoidal shape suddenly dominate the horizon in front of you. Stay on this small trail until you reach the closest corner of Jicarita. The trail itself contours around the south and west sides of Jicarita and meets the trail coming up from Indian Creek at the northwest corner of Jicarita. Get off the trail and walk up the southeast corner of Jicarita. If you watch closely you will find patches of trail going up through the scree and grass of the slope. Soon you will be on the flat, wide top, with vistas in all directions, and several rock shelters if you want to eat your lunch out of the ever-present wind. The southern horizon is particularly awesome, with the jagged Truchas Peaks and the gentler slopes of Trampas and Chimayosos Peaks dominating the skyline. Always observe caution when up on the Divide and watch for storm clouds; summer thunderstorms can roll in fast and you do not want to be above timberline when the lightning starts striking.

Return the way you came. As you near the post without its sign on the ridge, you may find it harder to follow the cairns and the patches of trail. Veer slightly down (southeast) instead of staying at contour, or you will end up in a large pile of scree.

Note: If you want to make this into a backpack trip, Serpent Lake is an ideal campsite halfway up the trail. It is situated in a lovely grassy meadow and you can set your tent up in the dwarfed trees just north of the lake, then proceed on up to Jicarita Peak. Weather permitting, you can return to the divide the next day and walk in the other direction, to the southwest, following sketchy trails along the top of the Santa Barbara Divide and drinking in the magnificent 360-degree views. (I do not know why the lake got its name, other than that several little grassy hummocks in the lake look rather like a small serpent swimming along, when viewed from the trail above.)

NORTH

Tetilla Peak

Draw

"Tank #28" Sign

Tetilla Peak

"800' Well" Sign

1 MILE

kH

118

TETILLA PEAK

by
Ingrid Vollnhofer

U.S. GEOLOGICAL SURVEY MAP REQUIRED: Tetilla Peak -
7.5 minute series.

SALIENT FEATURES: Tetilla Peak is a prominent volcano on
the Caja del Rio Plateau, a volcanic field formed some 2.6 million
years ago. An open area with a lot of cholla cactus and juniper.
Wonderful panorama from Tetilla Peak of Mount Taylor and the
Jemez, Taos, Sangre de Cristo, Ortiz, and Sandia Mountains.
There is a lot of cactus on the way, so hiking boots are recommended. The last six miles of driving are on a rough, rutted road,
which will be muddy and probably impassable during or after wet
weather. A vehicle with high clearance will make this drive less
scary. Bring plenty of water.

RATING: Easy but steep.

ROUND TRIP HIKING DISTANCE: 2.5 miles. Add 2.8 miles
if the last stretch of road is too rough for your car.

APPROXIMATE ROUND TRIP HIKING TIME: 2-3 hours,
including breathing, vista, water and snack breaks.

ALTITUDE RANGE: Highest point, 7206 feet; lowest point, 6260
feet; cumulative uphill hiking, 946 feet.

119

SEASONAL CONSIDERATIONS: Pretty hot in summer.

ROUND TRIP DRIVING: 36 miles; approximately 2 hours.

DRIVING DIRECTIONS: Take Cerrillos Road south from downtown Santa Fe. Turn right onto Airport Road. Measure your mileage from this turn. Tetilla Peak is visible straight ahead of you. After driving about 3 miles on Airport Road, you will come to a stop sign. Beyond this intersection, Airport Road branches off to the left, but you keep driving straight ahead. You are now on County Road #56. Continue past the sewage treatment plant (hold your nose!) and then past a large red scoria boulder. At 6.6 miles, look for a road coming in from the right. In June 1994, this road was marked by three signs: "Rancho Oso Rio," "Soccer," and "RC." Turn right here. This graded dirt road crosses a cattle guard, then climbs the hill to the left. At the top (7.6 miles), when the road turns sharply to the right, you drive straight ahead onto a rough, primitive road. (For a good winter strenuous hike, you can park here, walk the power line and head for Tetilla Peak. This is about 12 miles round trip.)

About a quarter of a mile after you drive onto the small dirt road, a branch road takes off to the right in the direction of the power line. Ignore it and all various turnouts and continue on the obvious road. You come to a "Y" and continue straight, swinging left around the rutty dip. At 8.4 miles the road passes between two large posts. You go through one cattle guard after this, at 8.7 miles. At 12.1 miles you come to a fence line and a sign that says "800 well, Santa Fe 21, Trail 24." Turn right here. Stop and check the road that follows the fence toward Tetilla Peak. How deep are the ruts, how high the tumbleweed piles? If the road looks bad, park your car here and start walking toward Tetilla Peak. If you can, drive another 1.4 miles on this road to a fork. Turn left at a battered "Tank 28" sign and park.

HIKING INSTRUCTIONS: There is no trail. This walk is a free-for-all. Head for Tetilla Peak in front of you. There is no other peak around. Avoid the draw which you see ahead of you. Keep to the left of it and stay high. While climbing, look back and note some distant high landmark in the direction of your car to guide you on the way down. It is easier to go off course than this open landscape would lead you to believe. At the very last stretch, the walk is quite steep, almost a scramble. Don't forget, the view at the top is magnificent.

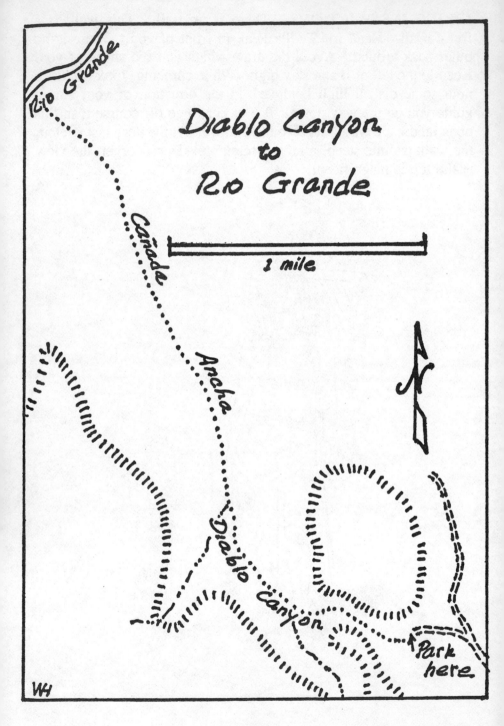

Diablo Canyon
to
Rio Grande

1 mile

Rio Grande

Cañada

Ancha

Diablo Canyon

N

Park
here.

WH

DIABLO CANYON TO RIO GRANDE

by
Polly Robertson and Norbert Sperlich

Note: This is a variation of the hike first suggested and written up by Polly Robertson for the earlier editions of the book.

U.S. GEOLOGICAL SURVEY MAP REQUIRED: White Rock - 7.5 minute series. On the map, Diablo Canyon is called Caja del Rio Canyon.

SALIENT FEATURES: This hike takes you through a short but spectacular canyon with vertical walls of basalt, and continues along a sandy arroyo to the Rio Grande. There are great views all along the way. The access road is poorly maintained and can be very rough. Four-wheel drive and a high clearance are an advantage when road conditions are less than perfect.

RATING: Easy.

ROUND TRIP HIKING DISTANCE: 6 miles.

APPROXIMATE ROUND TRIP HIKING TIME: 3 hours.

ALTITUDE RANGE: Highest point 5850 feet; lowest point 5450 feet; cumulative uphill hiking, 400 feet.

SEASONAL CONSIDERATIONS: Too hot in summer, unless you go early in the morning. Road may not be passable after heavy rain or snow.

ROUND TRIP DRIVING: About 36 miles; 1 hour 40 minutes or longer, depending on road conditions.

DRIVING DIRECTIONS: Take Washington Avenue north from the plaza. Turn left in front of the pink-stuccoed Scottish Rite Temple onto Paseo de Peralta. At the intersection with Guadalupe Street, turn right onto Guadalupe, which joins Highway #84/285. Continue north on #84/285 to Camino la Tierra on your left just past the concrete median wall. This is about 2.5 miles from the plaza. Turn left onto Camino la Tierra. Take your mileage at the turnoff. You will be driving on this road (which eventually becomes Buckman Road) for about 15.5 miles. The first 5.5 miles are paved and take you to the La Tierra development. Occasionally, the road splits, and there will be trees and bushes separating the two lanes. Stay in the right lane and go straight ahead at intersections. Once you come to the unpaved part of the road, you will encounter washboard surface, cattle guards, and ruts or deep sand where the road is crossed by drainages. Slow down!

About 11 miles from the turnoff onto Camino la Tierra, you will pass a windmill (Dead Dog Well) and a corral on your left. Take a mileage reading here. At this point a wide arroyo (Cañada Ancha) comes in from the left. This arroyo follows the edge of the Caja del Rio volcanic field. The latter is now visible on your left, forming a basalt-capped escarpment. The road stays to the right of the escarpment, going downhill over sandy terrain. Soon, the vertical cliffs of Diablo Canyon will appear ahead of you to the left. The canyon separates a small mesa that is edged by basalt cliffs from the lava mesa to the west. At 4.3 miles from the windmill look for a secondary road that branches off to the left and toward Diablo Canyon. Take this road to an open area close to the mouth of the canyon. Park your car here.

124

HIKING INSTRUCTIONS: Head toward the arroyo that goes into the canyon. You will have to cross a fence. At the entrance of the canyon, vertical cliffs rise up some 300 feet. As you go deeper into the canyon, you will notice that the basalt columns rest on sand and gravel -- a very unstable foundation, indeed. About ten minutes into the hike, you will come to a place where water is seeping out of the ground. To the right of this spot, where basalt columns form an overhang, cliff swallows like to build their nests. In the summertime, you can see swallows feeding their young. The unique descending scale call of the canyon wren can often be heard here. Soon, the canyon widens and, on your right and toward the top of the mesa, basalt cliffs give way to layers of ashes and cinders that have been eroded into jagged shapes.

As you walk out of the canyon, the arroyo widens and heads north for a while, toward Buckman Mesa. The arroyo soon swerves left (northwest) and descends slowly toward the Rio Grande. If you look skyward once in a while, you may see hawks or ravens circling above. Ahead of you, on the other side of the (still hidden) Rio Grande, you will see dark basalt cliffs topped by orange tuff. The basalt comes from the Caja del Rio volcanoes; the tuff was produced by eruptions of the Jemez caldera. After hiking a little over an hour, you will come to the river. From this point look upstream toward Buckman Mesa and its small peak. Does it look like a hound dog or a crocodile in profile? Had you been here around the turn of the century, you would have encountered a bridge crossing the river, a railroad line, and a settlement built by lumberman Henry Buckman. It's all gone now. The Buckman area is important for Santa Fe, however, because here are wells that produce part of the water supply.

Return to your car the way you came. Yes, it is hotter now, you are going uphill, and walking in the sand seems to be more tiresome. But once again you will enter Diablo Canyon and can find a shady spot to linger a while, before you drive back to Santa Fe.

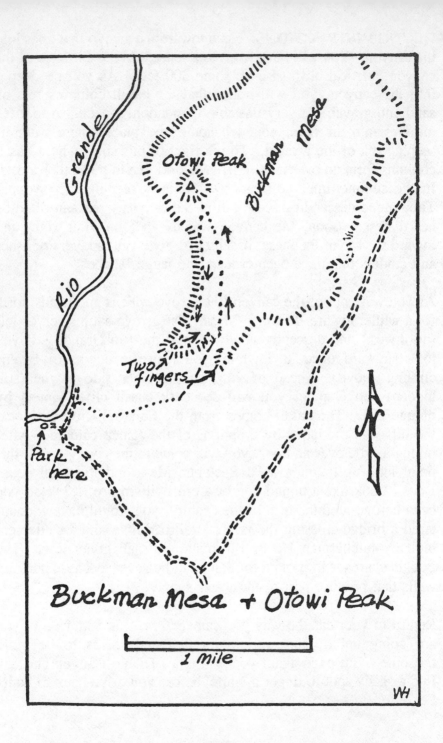

Grande

Rio

Otowi Peak

Buckman Mesa

Two fingers

Park here

1 mile

Buckman Mesa + Otowi Peak

WH

126

BUCKMAN MESA - OTOWI PEAK

by
Polly Robertson and Norbert Sperlich

Note: This is a variation of the hike first suggested and written up by Polly Robertson for the earlier editions of this book.

U.S. GEOLOGICAL SURVEY MAP REQUIRED: White Rock - 7.5 minute series.

SALIENT FEATURES: Buckman Mesa is the isolated mesa south of Otowi Bridge that guards the entrance to White Rock Canyon. Most of the mesa top is flat except for its western corner, where Otowi Peak, the remnant of a volcano, rises 1100 feet above the Rio Grande. The peak offers magnificent views in all directions.

Most of the hike goes over rough terrain. There are no trails on top of the mesa. Do not attempt this hike unless you are confident of your route-finding abilities. The access road can be very rough, rutted and/or muddy, especially after rain or snow. Four-wheel drive and a high clearance are a great advantage when road conditions are less than perfect. Bring water, at least a quart per person in hot weather.

RATING: Moderate.

ROUND TRIP HIKING DISTANCE: 5½ miles.

APPROXIMATE ROUND TRIP HIKING TIME: 4 hours.

ALTITUDE RANGE: Highest point, 6547 feet; lowest point, 5450 feet; cumulative uphill hiking, 1100 feet.

SEASONAL CONSIDERATIONS: Too hot in summer. Road may not be passable after heavy rain or snow.

ROUND TRIP DRIVING: 42 miles; about 2 hours.

DRIVING DIRECTIONS: Take Washington Avenue north from the plaza. Turn left in front of the pink Scottish Rite Temple onto Paseo de Peralta. At the intersection with Guadalupe Street, turn right and follow Guadalupe which joins US #84/285. Continue north on #84/285 to Camino la Tierra on your left just past the median wall, about 2.5 miles from the plaza. Turn left onto Camino la Tierra. Take your mileage at the turnoff. You will be driving on this road (which eventually becomes Buckman Road) all the way down to the Rio Grande. The first 5.5 miles are paved and take you to the La Tierra development. Occasionally, the road splits, and there will be trees and bushes separating the two lanes. Stay in the right lane and go straight ahead at intersections. On the unpaved section of the road, you will encounter washboard surface, cattle guards, and ruts or deep sand where the road is crossed by drainages. Slow down!

About 11 miles from the turnoff onto Camino la Tierra, you will pass a windmill and a corral on your left. Your road now parallels Cañada Ancha (a sandy arroyo) and the basalt-capped edge of the Caja del Rio volcanic field on the left. Soon, the vertical walls of Diablo Canyon (called Caja del Rio Canyon on the topo map) will appear ahead of you to the left. At 15.5 miles, you will pass the turnoff (on the left) to Diablo Canyon. Further down the road, ignore roads that go off to the right or left. Drive slowly and look for ruts. The last few road miles can be bad! A grove of tamarisks ahead will tell you that the river is near. Shortly after the Rio Grande comes in sight, the road turns left and up to an open spot. Park your car here. You have driven 18.5 miles from the La Tierra turnoff.

HIKING INSTRUCTIONS: Before starting the hike, you may want to spend a few minutes at the bank of the river. Its muddy waters are always a welcome sight in this dry country. Upstream, to your right, Buckman Mesa rises steeply. No trail going up is to be seen from here. This hike will take you to the southern end of the mesa. There, Buckman Mesa ends in two long "fingers," and a rough trail climbs up to the mesa top between the two fingers.

First, go back on the road that you just drove on. While still in the tamarisk grove, look for a secondary road that goes off to the left (north). Follow this road for about 5 minutes to a fence (with a gate) and some 30 yards beyond the fence to a wide arroyo. Follow the arroyo upstream. Soon it narrows into a canyon with vertical walls of compacted sand. After hiking in the arroyo for about 8 minutes, you may have to cross a fence. (Sometimes the fence is rolled back.) A few minutes later, you will come to a place where the arroyo turns to the right. On your left is a vertical wall of sand. Some 30 yards further, you will see a much eroded trail going up on the left. It is usually marked by cairns. If you miss the trail, you will see a small drainage coming in from the left at ground level, creating a break in the canyon wall and affording you a glimpse of the southern tip of Buckman Mesa. You have gone too far! Go back about 30 yards and look for the trail.

The first part of the trail is rough and getting worse every year, due to erosion. Look for "ducks" (small rocks placed on top of larger rocks) and footprints if you lose sight of the trail. The general direction is up, keeping the drainage on your right. After about half an hour of climbing, you are close to the top of the mesa. Just before you reach the mesa top, the trail moves into the drainage and then to the right side of it. Look around when you reach the top. You will have to find this place on your way back.

Otowi Peak is not yet in sight, and the trail fizzles out. Keep going straight ahead. In a minute or so you will see the peak. Go for it! Occasionally you will have to make a detour to the right to avoid a steep gully.

Vegetation on the mesa consists of piñon and juniper bushes, sage, grasses, and flowers. September, when the snakeweed is blooming yellow, is my favorite time for this hike. November is great for watching the sandhill cranes fly south.

After hiking for about 20 minutes on the flat mesa top, you come to the cinder-strewn slope of Otowi Peak. Going up, take the path of least resistance and avoid the steep, rocky parts if possible. If, some 30 to 40 yards below the top, you come upon a faint, fairly level trail, you might want to follow it to the left (west). It leads to the blowhole, an opening dating back to the time when the volcano was spewing steam or hot gases. This entrance to the underworld is hidden from view behind rocks until you are very close to it. It is very dangerous and drops down steeply after a few yards, so keep out of the hole. Most likely, you will reach the top without having seen the blowhole.

Time to enjoy the views. To the west and southwest, the Rio Grande flows through White Rock Canyon, and the Jemez Mountains appear in the distance. Black Mesa can be seen to the northeast, and the Sangre de Cristos stretch across the horizon toward the east and northeast. Closer by, to the south, you will see the Caja del Rio volcanic field with its dark hills. Special note: Otowi Peak is just south of the San Ildefonso Indian Reservation boundary line, beyond which a permit is needed. Respect the land and do not wander any further north than the peak itself.

Before leaving the peak, take time to study your topo map and look at the terrain to the south. (Interesting note: the rocks on the peak are magnetic and compass readings will be inaccurate.) The trail that will take you down from the mesa top starts where the two "fingers" of the mesa meet. To get to this point, you will take a different route on the way back. Instead of heading straight for the trail, you will follow the western edge of the mesa all the way to the tip of the west "finger" and then you will continue along the east side of the finger to your trail. This route offers dramatic views into White Rock Canyon.

Leave the peak in a southerly direction and, after bypassing the first gully at the foot of the peak, head for the edge of the mesa on your right. Stay close to the edge, swerving left only to avoid steep drainages. Take time to look back once in a while. Awesome views of Otowi Peak and the canyon below!

Just before you reach the tip of the finger, you will come to a place where the mesa's edge on your right forms an overhang. Watch it! Some 40 minutes after leaving the peak, you should come to the tip of the finger. Turn left now, still following the edge of the mesa. You are heading toward the place where the two fingers join. Stay on top of the mesa, close to the edge. Soon the terrain descends a bit, and you will come to a drainage. Cross the drainage and remain on top of the mesa. Two or three minutes later, you will come to a second drainage. This drainage is your landmark. Look for a trail or cairns on the other side of the drainage and start heading down. (If you did not notice the second drainage and kept hiking along the edge of the mesa, you will soon end up at the tip of the second finger. Admire the great views, then go back along the edge and look for the drainage and/or cairns.) Go down the way you came up and back to your car.

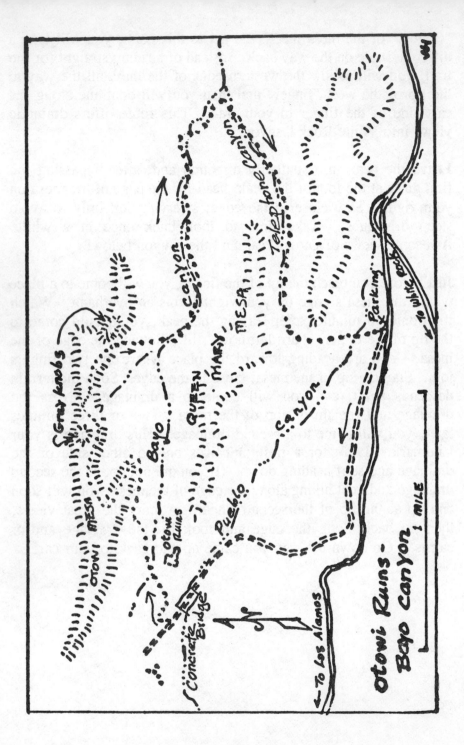

Otowi Ruins—
Bayo Canyon

1 MILE

OTOWI RUINS - BAYO CANYON

by
Arnold and Carolyn Keskulla

U.S. GEOLOGICAL SURVEY MAPS REQUIRED: Puye and, at the very beginning, White Rock - 7.5 minute series.

SALIENT FEATURES: This hike takes you to the Pajarito Plateau east of the Jemez Mountains. The canyons and mesas in this area are carved out of Bandelier tuff (compacted volcanic ash). You willl find ancient ruins, cave dwellings, lovely views from mesa tops, pleasant walking in canyon bottoms, and beautiful seasonal flowers. Most of this hike is off trail, requiring shoes with good traction. It should not be attempted unless a member of the group is experienced in reading topo maps and is able to locate the position of the hikers on the map.

RATING: Moderate/strenuous.

ROUND TRIP HIKING DISTANCE: Eight miles.

APPROXIMATE ROUND TRIP HIKING TIME: Five hours, with stops.

ALTITUDE RANGE: Highest point, 6800 feet; lowest point, 6100 feet; cumulative uphill hiking, 900 feet.

SEASONAL CONSIDERATIONS: Spring, fall, winter if not too much snow. Probably too hot in midsummer.

133

ROUND TRIP DRIVING: 57 miles; 1½ hours.

DRIVING DIRECTIONS: From the plaza, drive north on Washington Avenue to Paseo de Peralta. Turn left at the light in front of the pink Scottish Rite Temple. Proceed on Paseo de Peralta to the next stoplight, at Old Taos Highway, and turn right. In about 1.8 miles, Old Taos Highway merges with US #84/285. Drive north on #84/285 about 13.5 miles to where State Road #502 forks left toward Los Alamos. Take this left (west) fork. SR #502 crosses the Rio Grande and climbs to a well-marked "Y" intersection about 28 miles from Santa Fe. The right leg of the "Y," which you do not take, goes to Bandelier National Monument and White Rock. Go straight ahead (left leg of the "Y") toward Los Alamos for 0.3/mile. Turn right into a paved road leading off toward two gates and a maintenance yard. Park before the left gate, leaving enough room for large trucks to get by. The hikers' entrance is to the right of this gate.

HIKING INSTRUCTIONS: Go through the hikers' gate and follow the gravel road northwesterly through ponderosa pines with a view of Chicoma Peak ahead. The road heads uphill for a while, then drops down into Pueblo Canyon. Notice a funny smell? The little stream on your right originates at the Los Alamos sewage treatment plant. About 1.75 miles (40 minutes) into the hike, the road crosses the stream. Look to your right. About 30 yards past the bridge, you will see an old jeep trail going off to the right into the trees. This turnoff may be marked by a small cairn. Turn right here. Immediately after the turnoff, the trail passes between two small boulders and snakes up a low ridge that separates Pueblo Canyon from Bayo Canyon. In about 5 minutes you will come to the top of the ridge and a "T" junction with another trail. Turn right. The trail stays on the ridge top and leads in another 5 minutes to the fenced-in ruin of Otowi Pueblo (inhabited from the 1300s to the 1500s).

The ruin has been excavated and backfilled. What you can see now are mounds of rubble covered with weeds. However, go to the highest part of the site to appreciate the beautiful setting. To the east, the pueblo dwellers could see the Truchas Peaks; to the west, Pajarito and Caballo Mountain. To the north, the cliff face of Otowi Mesa towers over Bayo Canyon. Note the numerous cave cliff dwellings at the base of the cliffs; they are your next destination.

When you leave the ruins, follow the fence on your right (north) to the edge of the ridge. There, turn left and follow the edge for 15 yards. You will see two boulders on your right. A steep trail goes down between these boulders, taking you into Bayo Canyon. Go downstream (east) on the sandy bottom. After about 300 feet, and before a sharp bend in the arroyo, go up the bank on the left and angle northeast. If you are observant, you will see a ground-level pueblo ruin among the trees. Go north up the hillside toward the cliffs. If a mere dozen caves will do, cut to the right halfway up the hill and bear for a point near the corner of the cliffs. There is a game trail that you might find.

At the base of the cliffs are many soot-blackened caves with viga holes, Moki stairways, and accumulations of dung from burros and sheep. In front of this cliff there are also some lovely flowers in the late summer, such as Rocky Mountain bee plant, and an unusual white gilia with blue anthers (ipomopsis polyanthis). When you come to the pointed end of the mesa, go around it and follow the cliff face on the other side (in a northwesterly direction). After hiking about 100 yards (5 minutes), you will come to a place that is usually marked by small cairns. Here you can get on top of the cliffs that form the vertical edge of the mesa. (Mark this place if you want to return this way instead of completing the hike as described.) Follow the edge of the mesa.

You will see to the northwest that this mesa joins another which has two large gray domes. Stay at the level you are on, heading

135

northwest until you can follow the level around to the gray-domed mesa. Proceed eastward toward the first gray dome. Wind and water have sculpted it into rounded forms. After climbing the first dome, continue eastward. The mesa becomes very narrow, then widens again. Stay on the right (south rim) side. A little more than halfway between the first and second domes, there is a break in the cliff face (marked in February 1994 with cairns and tree branches). This is where you go down -- in a little while.

First, continue on to the second gray dome to enjoy the sweeping views: to the east and northeast, the Sangre de Cristos span the horizon. More to the north are the Taos and Latir mountains. The Jemez Mountains appear to the west. The nearby mesa south of you is the "Queen Mary" Mesa, presumably named after the ocean liner. Further to the south are the dark hills of the Caja del Rio volcanic fields, and in the distance the Sandia Mountains.

Time to go back. As you head west, with the mesa edge on your left, look for the break in the cliffs (about 100 yards after you leave the smooth gray rock). It is much easier to see approaching this way. Down you go. After a short rock scramble, you will be on the sloping shoulder of the mesa.

Angle steeply down (south) over the loose rocks to a small sandy-bottomed canyon that soon joins Bayo Canyon. From this junction continue down Bayo Canyon (east) for about 1.5 miles (approximately 30 minutes) to the first major arroyo coming in from the right. At the junction, look for cairns. Looking up the canyon coming in from the right, you will see the narrow end of the "Queen Mary" mesa. Go up this winding side canyon for about half an hour, until you come to a trail that climbs out of the arroyo to the left. This trail follows a telephone line. Stay on this trail until it reaches the ridge top. To your left (south) you will see the Los Alamos road. Leave the trail and head toward that road, in the direction of a white water tower, visible above the road. In a few minutes you will reach the bottom of Pueblo Canyon and the little stream. Now the maintenance yard should be clearly visible. Keep it to your left while you go up the road where you started your hike, and back to your car.

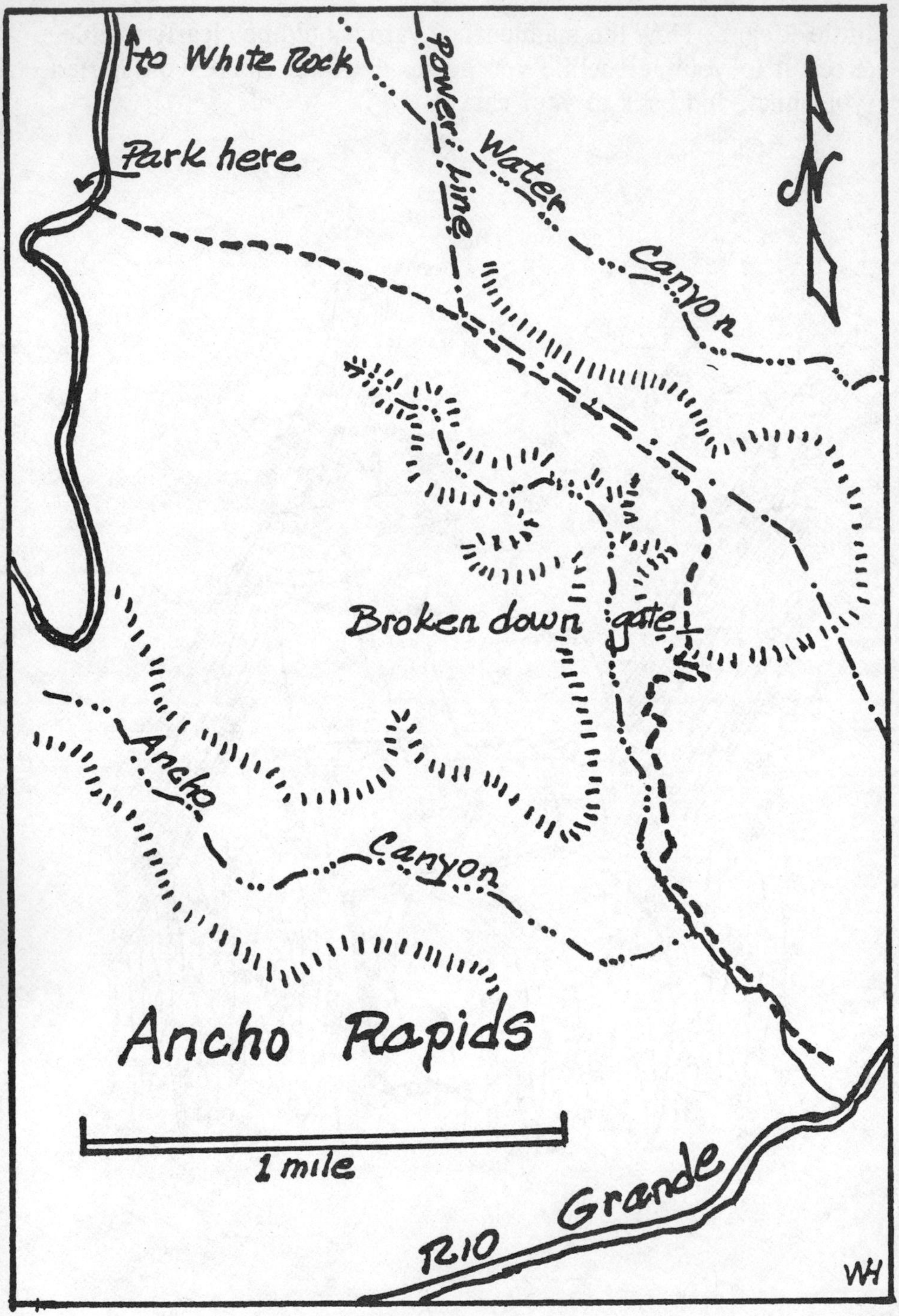

to White Rock

Park here

Power line

Water Canyon

N

Broken down gate

Ancho

Canyon

Ancho Rapids

1 mile

Rio Grande

WH

138

ANCHO RAPIDS

by
Bill and Linda Zwick

U.S. GEOLOGICAL SURVEY MAP REQUIRED: White Rock - 7.5 minutes series.

SALIENT FEATURES: A pleasant hike to the bottom of White Rock Canyon. It starts in a piñon forest, proceeds through concentrations of juniper and yucca, and then descends steeply into scenic Ancho Canyon. There you will follow a little stream down to the Rio Grande. Sturdy shoes are recommended. Cacti abound, so people and dogs should be careful not to get spines in their feet.

RATING: Moderate.

ROUND TRIP HIKING DISTANCE: About 6 miles.

APPROXIMATE ROUND TRIP HIKING TIME: 3 hours, stops not included.

ALTITUDE RANGE: Highest point, 6500 feet; lowest point, 5460 feet; cumulative uphill hiking, 1040 feet.

SEASONAL CONSIDERATIONS: Potentially very hot in summer and may be slippery when wet or after snowfall, but generally a year-round hike.

ROUND TRIP DRIVING: About 74 miles; 1½ hours.

DRIVING DIRECTIONS: From the plaza, drive north on Washington Avenue to Paseo de Peralta. Turn left at the light in front of the pink Scottish Rite Temple. Proceed on Paseo de Peralta to the next stoplight, at Old Taos Highway, and turn right. In about 1.8 miles, Old Taos Highway merges with US #84/285. Drive north on #84/285 about 13.5 miles to where State Road #502 forks left toward Los Alamos. Take this left (west) fork. SR #502 crosses the Rio Grande and climbs to a well-marked "Y" intersection. The left leg of this "Y" (which you do not take) goes to Los Alamos. Take the right leg toward Bandelier and White Rock. About 1.5 miles from the "Y" is a stoplight where the truck route to Los Alamos and the road to the Pajarito Ski Area go right. You drive straight ahead through this light toward White Rock and Bandelier. Five miles from the "Y," you arrive at White Rock's only traffic signal (the intersection with Pajarito Road). Carefully check your odometer reading here and drive on straight through the traffic signal, still heading south. Continue on toward Bandelier National Monument for about 3.4 miles.

As you approach a yellow diamond-shaped sign indicating that the road will turn left (the third such sign after White Rock), look for a gate on the left side of the road. There is a gravelled parking area and a metal "Notice" sign in front of this gate. The gate is identified as No. 4. You might find it necessary to pull off on the right shoulder of the road (the road is narrow here) to see the gate and the small graveled parking area. Traffic in this area moves rapidly around blind curves, so take appropriate care in pulling into the parking area. (If you have taken a hair-pin curve to the left over an arroyo and then up a moderate hill to find a gate, you've gone too far! If the walking entrance through the fence is a simple opening, you are at the wrong gate and you should go back 0.2/mile toward White Rock.) The large gate will probably be locked due to a recent DOE crack-down on motor vehicle traffic in the area. Pedestrian access is through an entrance to the right of the large gate. This entrance forms a sharp angle to prevent the passage of cattle.

140

HIKING INSTRUCTIONS: Proceed through the angled pedestrian access. The hike to the rim of the canyon follows a road built for the installation of powerlines in the area. This portion of the hike toward the Rio Grande provides spectacular vistas of the Sangre de Cristo mountains (especially nice in the fall when the aspen are golden) and the return provides nice views of the Jemez Mountains and Bandelier. You will cross under a powerline which heads north and south, and about a mile into the hike the road will converge with another powerline which heads east. Note the radio telescope dish to your right (south) -- this Los Alamos facility is part of an array of radio telescopes stretching from the South Pacific to the continental U.S. Continue walking on the road eastward. Looking down, you might notice large ant hills shimmering in the sunlight -- a result of the ants' mining quartz grains to make their homes.

About 1.75 miles from the start of the hike, the road will descend and then begin to rise toward the canyon rim. Shortly after you begin ascending, a road branches off to the right (southeast). Take this spur to its end (approximately 0.5/mile). At this point you are at the rim of Ancho Canyon. Note the broken-down fence and gate which once prevented cattle from descending into the canyon to graze. Bear to your right (toward the sandstone cliff) and you will find a trail winding through rockfall which will then begin a steep traverse to the bottom of the canyon. The trail shows little sign of use, is eroded and rocky in places, but is easy to follow.

At the bottom of the canyon, the trail is mostly obvious, but cairns aid your travel here. When the canyon bottom levels out, you will find a spring-fed stream to your right. It's a nice place to rest after your climb down or before beginning your climb back up. The authors shared this rest spot with a large, but shy, black bear! The river is not far from here and the trail and cairns will take you to the water's edge.

You can explore the bank of the river for varying distances, depending on the water level. Note the dead tamarisk and oak high on the river banks -- a result of the high water level of Cochiti Reservoir several years ago. Rocks and debris washed from Ancho Canyon in flash floods have formed Ancho ("wide" in Spanish) Rapid, the most difficult rapid in White Rock Canyon for the river runners who boat past.

To return, retrace your steps. On the way back up the scree slope, notice the huge cholla next to a large old log at the corner of one of the switchbacks. And pick up a large piece of the pumice which is so light; if you have a camera, get a companion to take a photograph of you as you heft massive rocks with ease.

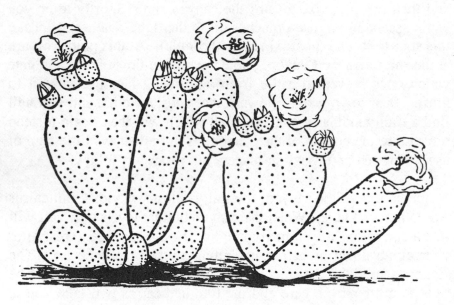

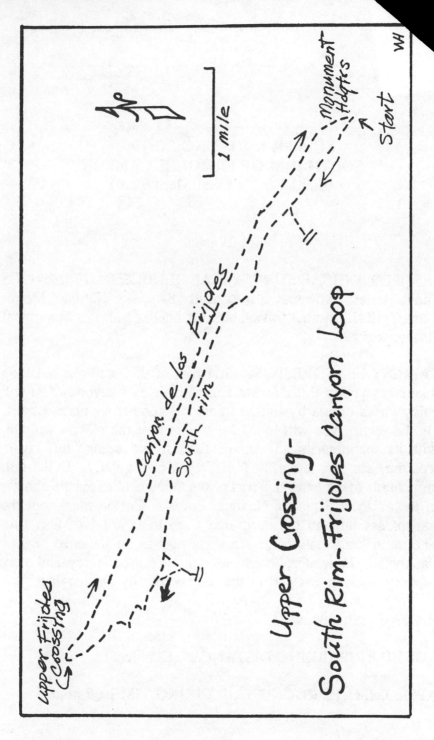

Upper Crossing-
South Rim-Frijoles Canyon Loop

Upper Frijoles Crossing

Canyon de los Frijoles

South rim

Monument Hdqtrs

Start

1 mile

UPPER CROSSING LOOP -
SOUTH RIM OF FRIJOLES CANYON
(Bandelier National Monument)

by
Joe Whelan

U.S. GEOLOGICAL SURVEY MAP REQUIRED: Frijoles - 7.5 minute series. You may also consult "Bandelier National Monument, Trails Illustrated," available at Bandelier National Monument Headquarters.

SALIENT FEATURES: The first part of this well-marked loop hike takes you to the southern rim of Frijoles Canyon. You will enjoy views of nearby Indian ruins and distant mountain ranges. On the return, you will hike at the bottom of the narrow canyon, with its sparkling stream, mixed forests, and orange tuff cliffs. You may see deer along the trail, if you hike quietly. In the fall, large herds of elk enter this part of the monument to escape hunters in the adjacent Santa Fe National Forest. On the mesa top, the trail passes through the burn area from the 1977 La Mesa fire. The return trail features 25 stream crossings on flattened logs or flat rocks. In winter, these crossings are usually icy and very slippery, making this part of the loop especially challenging.

RATING: Strenuous.

ROUND TRIP HIKING DISTANCE: 13 miles.

APPROXIMATE ROUND TRIP HIKING TIME: 7 hours.

ALTITUDE RANGE: Highest point, 7400 feet; lowest point, 6066 feet; cumulative uphill hiking, 1600 feet.

SEASONAL CONSIDERATIONS: Can be uncomfortably hot in midsummer. In winter, the mesa top is usually lightly snow-covered or muddy, and the stream crossings are icy. Most beautiful during the late fall.

ROUND TRIP DRIVING: 92 miles; 2-2½ hours.

DRIVING DIRECTIONS: From the plaza, drive north on Washington Avenue to Paseo de Peralta. Turn left at the light in front of the pink Scottish Rite Temple. Proceed on Paseo de Peralta to the next stoplight, at Old Taos Highway, and turn right. In about 1.8 miles, Old Taos Highway merges with US #84/285. Drive north on #84/285 about 13.5 miles to where State Road #502 forks left toward Los Alamos. Take this left (west) fork. SR #502 crosses the Rio Grande and climbs to a well-marked "Y" intersection. The left leg of this "Y" (which you do not take) goes to Los Alamos. Take the right leg toward Bandelier and White Rock. About 1.5 miles from the "Y" is a stoplight where the truck route to Los Alamos and the Pajarito Ski Area go right. You drive straight ahead through this light toward White Rock and Bandelier. The entrance to Bandelier is about 12.5 miles from the "Y." There is an entrance fee. Drive to the Visitors Center and across the bridge over the Rio Frijoles, turn left, and park in the area designated for back country hikers.

HIKING INSTRUCTIONS: From the back country hikers' parking area across the bridge from the Visitors Center, walk back up the paved road past the bridge about 50 yards to a posted map and sign indicating the trails to Stone Lions and Frijolito Ruin. Take the trail behind the sign about 100 feet to a junction and second sign. Follow the sign for the Stone Lions Trail to the right (northwest) for a quarter of a mile to another junction and sign, where you will turn left onto the uphill switchback Stone Lions Trail to the top of

Frijoles Canyon's south rim. On this portion of the trail there are good view of the ruins in and on the north side of Frijoles Canyon, and from the top of the rim you can see the Ceremonial Cave and the long ladders leading up to it, directly across the canyon.

At the top of the rim, follow the sign for Upper Crossing to the right, and at the junction several yards further on follow the second sign to Upper Crossing (5 miles) to the right (northwest). The trail first passes along the Canyon's south rim, then through a small wooded draw, and after about a mile reaches the mesa top, where you will hike through sparsely wooded meadows with mountain views in all directions for the next 5 miles. About 2 miles along the mesa top, the trail enters the 1977 burn area.

The next trail junction is about 3.5 miles from the junction and second sign to Upper Crossing; you continue to the right (west), following the sign to Upper Crossing and, about a quarter-mile further on, another junction, where you again continue to the right (northwest), now following the trail to Ponderosa Campground (3.1 miles). After about a half-mile gradual climb, the trail descends into a wooded draw and the Upper Crossing in Frijoles Canyon. This makes a good place for lunch. At the Upper Crossing signpost, take the trail toward Ponderosa Campground for about 50 feet and over the log bridge across Frijoles Creek. Here is a small clearing that is usually sunny even in winter and has several large rocks to rest on while you take a break.

After this detour to the clearing, cross back over the creek to the Upper Crossing signpost. Return to the Visitors Center by following the sign at Upper Crossing to the Park Headquarters (6 miles) downstream. This return trail through the narrow canyon bottom and along the stream is bordered by steep, colorful rock formations and is heavily wooded. There are no junctions along the 6 miles of return trail, but there are 25 stream crossings, most of them with primitive bridges. At the Ceremonial Cave ruins, about one mile from the Visitors Center, the trail widens to a

146

nature trail and finally reaches the paved picnic grounds road and back country hikers' parking area.

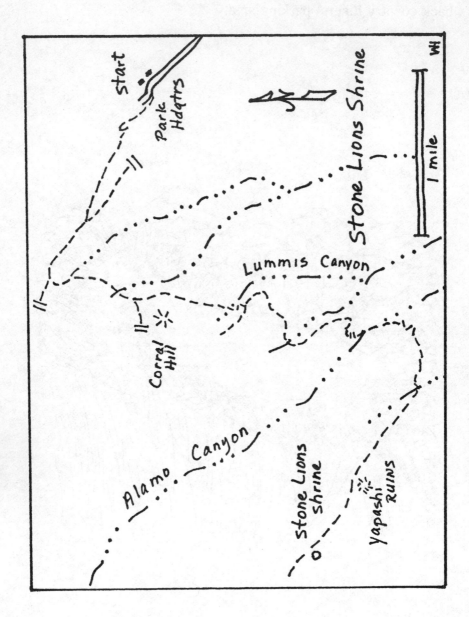

Start

Park Hdqtrs

Stone Lions Shrine

N

1 mile

Lummis Canyon

Corral Hill

Alamo Canyon

Stone Lions Shrine

Yapashi Ruins

148

STONE LIONS SHRINE
(Bandelier National Monument)

by
Mickey Bogert

U.S. GEOLOGICAL SURVEY MAP REQUIRED: Frijoles - 7.5 minute series.

SALIENT FEATURES: This is a challenging walk to an ancient shrine showing signs of current use by Indians from the nearby pueblos. It is a strenuous hike because of the climbs in and out of several beautiful canyons, especially Alamo.

The walks across the mesa tops are easy, on good trails, with views of the Sangre de Cristo and Jemez Mountains. Vegetation is mostly piñon-juniper with some ponderosa pine. Just before the Stone Lions Shrine is a large, unexcavated pueblo ruin. Note: It is unlawful to remove anything from the National Monument, especially Indian artifacts. No dogs are allowed in the National Monument. Carry plenty of water.

RATING: Strenuous.

ROUND TRIP HIKING DISTANCE: 12.8 miles.

APPROXIMATE ROUND TRIP HIKING TIME: 8 hours.

ALTITUDE RANGE: Highest point, 6660 feet; lowest point, 6066 feet; cumulative uphill hiking, 2700 feet.

SEASONAL CONSIDERATIONS: Can be uncomfortably hot in summer.

ROUND TRIP DRIVING: 92 miles; approximately 2-2½ hours.

DRIVING DIRECTIONS: From the plaza, drive north on Washington Avenue to Paseo de Peralta. Turn left at the light in front of the pink Scottish Rite Temple. Proceed on Paseo de Peralta to the next stoplight, at Old Taos Highway, and turn right. In about 1.8 miles, Old Taos Highway merges with US #84/285. Drive north on #84/285 about 13.5 miles to where State Road #502 forks left toward Los Alamos. Take this left (west) fork. SR #502 crosses the Rio Grande and climbs to a well-marked "Y" intersection about 28 miles from Santa Fe. The left leg of the "Y" (which you do not take) goes to Los Alamos. Take the right leg, State Route #4, toward Bandelier and White Rock. About 1.5 miles from the "Y" is a stoplight where the truck route to Los Alamos and the road to the Pajarito Ski Area go right. You drive straight ahead through this light toward White Rock and Bandelier. The entrance to Bandelier is beyond White Rock about 12.5 miles from the "Y." There is an entrance fee. Drive to the Visitors Center and across the bridge over the Rio Frijoles, turn left, and park in the area designated for back country hikers.

HIKING INSTRUCTIONS: From the parking area, walk back up the paved road, past the bridge for a few hundred feet where you will see a sign on your left which will identify the trails to the Stone Lions and Frijolito Ruin. Turn left (southwest) onto this trail. The Stone Lions Trail soon branches from the Frijolito Ruin Trail and heads northwest (right). This is a fairly gradual climb and affords good views of the ruins in Frijoles Canyon. When you reach the top of the mesa you can see Ceremonial Cave, with the long ladders leading up to it, directly across the canyon. A few yards further on is a junction (1 mile from the Visitors Center). At this junction, follow the sign pointing left (south) to the Corral Hill-Stone Lions Trail.

Continue on the Stone Lions Trail, crossing Lummis Canyon (identified by a sign) and its two tributary canyons on each side of it, and then on to the rim of Alamo Canyon.

For most of this distance the vegetation is varied: juniper, piñon pine and some ponderosa, or yellow, pine, as well as yucca and cactus. The previous canyon crossings are semishaded and fairly easy, so Alamo Canyon comes as a shock, as well as a spectacular surprise. There are beautiful views, but no shade, and there is a very steep switchback trail down a precipitous cliff. It is essential to carry sufficient water, for it requires a great deal of effort to descend 500 feet in 0.3/mile and make a similar ascent on the other side. And you must do it again, in reverse, on the way back.

The canyon bottom does have trees, and a stream during certain times of the year. Do not drink the water. The trail goes downstream for several hundred yards before crossing and starting steeply upwards on the south side of the canyon. The south rim of the canyon is a good place for a snack break, to enjoy the view, and to gather strength for the next two miles. A half mile farther on is a shallow canyon, a tributary of Alamo, about 80 feet deep. The vegetation south of Alamo is quite different: more arid in appearance, no more ponderosa, and the junipers and piñons are shorter. Cactus is much more abundant.

(From here on, when snow covered, the trail may be difficult to follow.)

One mile beyond the little canyon, in a westerly direction, is Yapashi Pueblo, now a mound of rubble. From here you will have magnificent views of many mountains. To the west, the San Miguel Mountains; south, the Sandias; southeast, the Ortiz and San Pedro Mountains; northwest, the Jemez; and to the northeast, the Sangre de Cristo Mountains. A half mile beyond the Yapashi ruins, on your left, you will see a small enclosure made of piled-up stones. In the middle of this is what is left of the stone lion carvings. Time and the elements have obliterated the heads but the backs and haunches remain. Sometimes there are offerings of deer antlers hanging on the trees in back of the lions but more often antlers are racked around them, almost like a wreath. Most of us who come here sense a special atmosphere about this place. Remember that it is a sacred area, so please respect and enjoy it accordingly. Do not disturb any of the offerings.

Return to your car over the same trails.

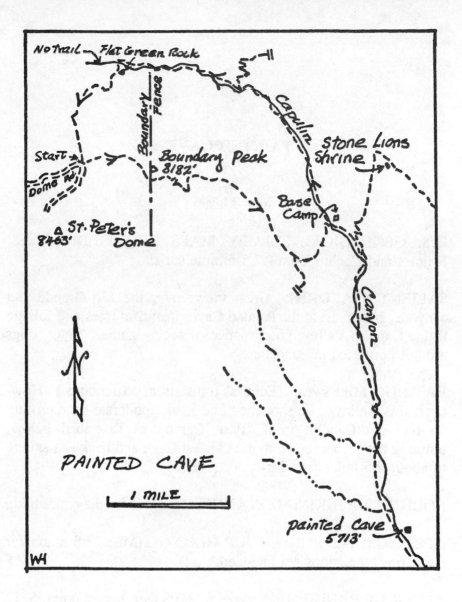

No Trail — Flat Green Rock

Boundary Fence

Start

Dome Rd.

△ St. Peter's
8463' Dome

Boundary Peak
8182'

Capulin

Stone Lions
Shrine

Base
Camp

Canyon

PAINTED CAVE

1 MILE

Painted Cave
5713'

W4

PAINTED CAVE

by
John Masters

U.S. GEOLOGICAL SURVEY MAPS REQUIRED: Bland, Frijoles and Cochiti Dam - 7.5 minute series.

SALIENT FEATURES: Great views over the Rio Grande and canyons; Indian art at the Painted Cave; beautiful trees and foliage in the Capulin Valley; good chance of seeing game. Note: dogs are not permitted in Bandelier.

RATING: Mild sweat. (Editors' translation: Strenuous.) However, this walk can be shortened and made moderate by returning up the Rio Capulin from "Base Camp" as described below, omitting the section down to the Painted Cave and back -- a saving of about 6.5 miles round trip.

ROUND TRIP HIKING DISTANCE: 15 miles for the entire hike.

APPROXIMATE ROUND TRIP HIKING TIME: 7-8 hours for the entire hike, stops not included.

ALTITUDE RANGE: Highest point, 8108 feet; lowest point, 5713 feet; cumulative uphill hiking, 2400 feet.

SEASONAL CONSIDERATIONS: Best in spring and fall. Impossible in winter unless very mild.

ROUND TRIP DRIVING: 97 miles; approximately 3¼ hours.

DRIVING DIRECTIONS: From the plaza, drive north on Washington Avenue to Paseo de Peralta. Turn left at the light in front of the pink Scottish Rite Temple. Proceed on Paseo de Peralta to the next stoplight, at Old Taos Highway, and turn right. In about 1.8 miles, Old Taos Highway merges with US #84/285. Drive north on #84/285 about 13.5 miles to where State Road #502 forks left toward Los Alamos. Take this left (west) fork. SR #502 crosses the Rio Grande and climbs to a well-marked "Y" intersection. Take the right branch toward White Rock and Bandelier. About 1.5 miles from the "Y," turn right at a traffic light. You are now on East Jemez Road. After about 5.7 miles, your road branches. Do not take the right lane that goes to Los Alamos. Keep straight ahead/slightly left through a series of traffic lights. In another 5.4 miles you will come to a "T" intersection with Route #4. This intersection is called the West Gate of Los Alamos. Turn right here, and check your odometer. The road winds and twists sharply and the scenery is beautiful, so drive carefully. About 6 miles from the West Gate you will come to Forest Road #289.

Turn left here and go straight past a sign reading "Leaving Bandelier" and over a cattle guard at 2.1 miles from where you turned onto #289. The cattle guard marks the Forest Service boundary. Note your odometer reading at this cattle guard. You have 8.6 miles more to go to reach the trailhead.

Stay on #289 until you come to another "T" junction. Take the left turn onto Forest Road #142. This junction will be about 5 miles from the cattle guard. Stay on FS #142 for 3.5 miles, ignoring several secondary roads to the left and right, and you will be at the trailhead. Park as the road turns sharply right and comes out on a steep edge overlooking the Rio Grande canyons. This is St. Peter's Dome Lookout Corner and the trailhead. Park to the left where there are signs indicating the trailhead. You will start down

155

Boundary Peak Trail #427 and return on Capulin Canyon Trail #116.

HIKING INSTRUCTIONS: This is a very beautiful walk, especially in fall, from the colors, and in spring, from the rush of water in the Capulin. Look for great cliff formations of tuff as you drop into Capulin Canyon; distant views of Chicoma and Caballo Mountains, and the Truchas Peaks across the whole valley; all three types of juniper -- common, Rocky Mountain and alligator; magnificent stands of ponderosa pine; hoof/paw marks and scats of black bear, deer, elk and wild burro (all these seem to use the area freely); tremendous views over Jemez canyons; fingerling trout in the Capulin; and, always, the half-hidden things -- the wildflowers, small animals, birds.

The walk is all down, then all up. If it's too hot, have a dip in the stream before starting the final ascent.

From the parking area, take Trail #427 heading, at that point, northeast (signposted); it turns east and wends down the side of Boundary Peak. After about one hour (altitude 6660 feet) you come to a junction signposted to Turkey Springs and Dome Lookout. Ignore the instructions, put your back to the sign and follow your trail north, down into Capulin Canyon (great views opposite). After about 15 minutes (altitude 6200 feet), cross the Rio Capulin at a large log building called, and signposted, "Base Camp." (Some maps may note this as a "Guard Station.") More signs here to be ignored as you continue right (southeast) down-stream. In 5 minutes you pass an Adirondack shelter on the left. From behind this, a trail (signposted) leads to the Stone Lions. Proceed on downstream, with several stream crossings (which are great fun in spring), for about another 45 minutes (altitude 5713 feet), where you will see the big scooped-out overhang of the Painted Cave to your left (northeast). A trail (signposted) takes off toward it, crossing the stream. Do not attempt to climb up to the

156

cave itself. It's dangerous and it's not allowed, to protect the art and the cave.

When you're ready to return, go back the same way you came as far as Base Camp. Do NOT cross the stream here, but continue north upstream past a sign reading "Trail." After about 45 minutes you come to a trail fork (altitude 6600 feet) where a trail goes off to the right. You follow the sign "Dome Lookout 3" and keep on going roughly west, up river. Thirty minutes later you reach the fence which shows that you are leaving Bandelier National Monument. About 15 minutes after that, at the first crossing of the Capulin after the boundary fence, cross to the true right bank (i.e., right when facing downstream) and look for the trail up the hill. There is a grey-green flat rock 7 by 12 feet in the clearing here. Go on 20 paces past it due south toward the slope. The trail takes off right (west-southwest) in the trees along the foot of the slope. It's difficult to miss this as there is no trail on up the river, after a hundred feet or so. Climb steadily, on a well-graded path with more great views, mostly behind you, to the cars; and you will find that you have come up on Capulin Canyon Trail #116.

Obviously this walk can be done in the reverse direction.

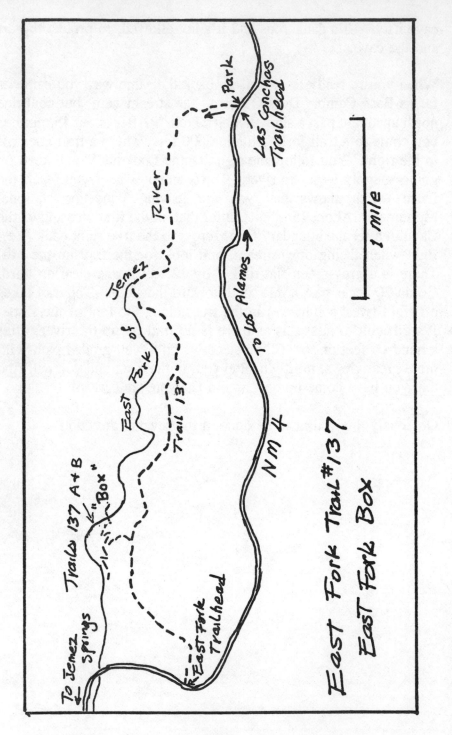

East Fork Trail #137
East Fork Box

To Jemez Springs
Trails 137 A+B
"Box"
East Fork of Jemez River
Trail 137
Park
Las Conchas Trailhead
To Los Alamos
NM 4
East Fork Trailhead

1 mile

EAST FORK TRAIL #137 - EAST FORK BOX
(Jemez National Recreation Area)

by
Tom Ribe

U.S. GEOLOGICAL SURVEY MAP REQUIRED: Redondo Peak - 7.5 minute series - 1977. This trail is not outlined on the map.

SALIENT FEATURES: A lovely hike beginning along the Jemez River as it passes through a canyon of blue spruce, fir, and pine growing among volcanic cliffs along a trail lined with wildflowers. The trail is well marked, with log and rail bridges over river crossings. After leaving the river, the trail winds through a pleasant mixed conifer and aspen forest.

The Jemez Mountains are the quiet remains of a field of volcanoes which erupted over many thousands of years. Two miles to the northwest of the trailhead, a large volcanic vent called El Cajete spewed light, chalky pumice into great drifts across the landscape about 60,000 years ago. This pumice, visible in road cuts but otherwise hidden beneath the mantle of forest soil, has been recently targeted by miners. The Jemez National Recreation Area was created by Congress in 1993, thanks to the efforts of the East Fork Preservation Coalition and the Sierra Club, to protect this area from pumice strip mining.

RATING: Moderate.

ROUND TRIP HIKING DISTANCE: 8 miles to East Fork Box and return; 9 miles on the main trail out-and-back; 4.5 miles if the main trail is hiked one way with a car shuttle.

APPROXIMATE ROUND TRIP HIKING TIME: 4-5 hours, depending on stops.

ALTITUDE RANGE: Highest point, 8560 feet; lowest point, 8080 feet on main trail, 8000 feet at East Fork Box; cumulative uphill hiking, 640 feet on main trail, 720 feet to East Fork Box.

SEASONAL CONSIDERATIONS: Spring through fall, depending on snow conditions.

ROUND TRIP DRIVING: 110 miles; about three hours, due to winding roads.

DRIVING DIRECTIONS: From the plaza, drive north on Washington Avenue to Paseo de Peralta. Turn left at the light in front of the pink Scottish Rite Temple. Proceed on Paseo de Peralta to the next stoplight, at Old Taos Highway, and turn right. In about 1.8 miles, Old Taos Highway merges with US #84/285. Drive north on #84/285 about 13.5 miles to where State Road #502 forks left toward Los Alamos. Take this left (west) fork. SR #502 crosses the Rio Grande and climbs to a well-marked "Y" intersection. Take the right branch toward White Rock and Bandelier. About 1.5 miles from the "Y," turn right at a traffic light. You are now on East Jemez Road. After about 5.7 miles, your road branches. Do not take the right lane that goes to Los Alamos. Keep straight ahead/slightly left through a series of traffic lights. In another 5.4 miles you will come to a "T" intersection with Route #4. This intersection is called the West Gate of Los Alamos. Turn right here, and check your odometer. The road winds and twists sharply and the scenery is beautiful, so drive carefully. The trailhead is 13.7 miles from the right turn.

Once in the Jemez Mountains, the road winds up along the Frijoles Canyon watershed until you drop down into the Valle Grande, the huge caldera and grassland surrounded by the Jemez peaks. The road then drops out of the Valle Grande and crosses the Jemez River at Las Conchas Campground. Half a mile farther, the road recrosses the river in an open area where a few houses stand on the left side of the road. Park in the gravel parking area on the right side of the road at the river crossing, directly across the road from a private driveway, and pass through the gate on the East Fork Trail to the north. This trailhead is called "Las Conchas" on the USFS signs.

HIKING DIRECTIONS: Begin hiking to the north following the river on the well-used trail, crossing on several log and rail bridges. The river meanders between steep canyon walls covered with an amazing variety of orange, chartreuse, pale green, and black lichens. Desert varnish trails over honeycomb patterns in the rock.

Though the canyon is beautiful, it bears the scars of decades of cattle grazing, which has denuded the streamside of much of its native vegetation, polluted the water, and eliminated many plant and bird species. Look for old beaver gnaw marks on some of the trees. Beaver were once plentiful here before cattle eliminated most of the willow thickets that provided the beavers' food and lodging material. Alert hikers may see dippers (water ouzels) along the stream, along with Steller's jays, western tanagers, and Rocky Mountain chickadees.

About two miles from the trailhead, the river leaves the meadow and forest bottom land and plunges in gentle falls into a box canyon where the cliffs fall directly into the water. At this point, at a cattle fence and gate, the river turns at nearly a right angle. The hiking trail leaves the river a few yards before the bend at trail signs noting that Las Conchas Trailhead (where you began) is 2 miles back and East Fork Trailhead is 3 miles farther on, to the left. The trail switches back up the north-facing slope in a 200-foot or so elevation gain to the ridgetop, passing through a wooden gate about one-third of the way up. At the top, Redondo Peak can now be seen directly to the north, with its forested ramparts and montane grasslands gleaming among aspen groves.

After arriving on the ridgetop, the trail continues through a logged forest of mixed conifer, New Mexican locust, and aspens. On the ridgetop, the forest tells the story of logging and fire suppression, which has changed it from open park lands of big trees before 1900 to the thickets of small trees that grow here today. After hiking 20 minutes on the ridgetop, the trail is crossed by a logging road. Shortly thereafter, it merges with a ski trail, the latter coming in from the left and marked by blue diamonds nailed to the trees. On occasion, the trail runs closely parallel to a logging road -- stay on the narrow trail!

Soon you will come to a trail junction marked by a sign. Trail #137 continues straight ahead to reach the East Fork Trailhead in a mile. Another trail (#137 A and B) goes off to the right and one-half mile down to the river. This right-hand trail soon branches. The right branch goes to the East Fork Box where the river leaves the box canyon. The trail makes a very steep descent to reach the river and cross a bridge. Head upstream after crossing the bridge to where the river comes out of a wild, rocky canyon. This spot makes an excellent lunch area and turn-around point for the hike. If you wish, follow the river upstream into the canyon (you will get your legs wet!) for 5 more minutes to a popular picnic area.

Rather than descending to the East Fork Box, you might choose instead to continue straight ahead from the junction on the main Trail #137 one more mile to the East Fork Trailhead. There you will find a wooden fence, parking area, outhouses, and the highway at the western East Fork trailhead.

Unless you are doing this hike as a shuttle, return on the main trail. About 20 minutes past the sign for the turnoff to the East Fork Box, the blue diamond ski trail separates from Trail #137 by veering off to the right (there is a lot of downed timber at this fork). Make sure you stay on the better defined hiking trail, to the left, to return to Las Conchas Trailhead and your car.

If your group has more than one car, you could arrange a car shuttle between the two highway trailheads -- Las Conchas and East Fork, which is 3.7 miles farther west on SR #4; this would cut the hiking distance in half.

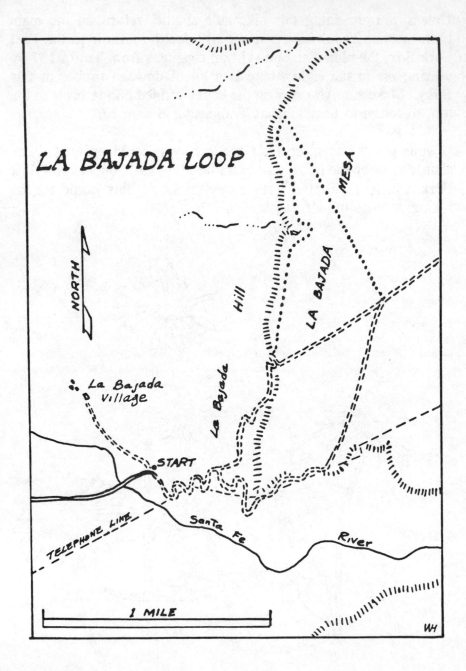

LA BAJADA LOOP

NORTH

MESA

LA BAJADA

Hill

La Bajada

La Bajada
village

START

TELEPHONE LINE

Santa Fe

River

1 MILE

WH

LA BAJADA LOOP

by
Bill Chudd

U.S. GEOLOGICAL SURVEY MAP REQUIRED: Tetilla Peak - 7.5 minutes series.

SALIENT FEATURES: An easy walk in open terrain with broad, spectacular views. Carry water, for there is none along the way. The approach to the trailhead is along a dirt road which may be muddy and impassable in very wet weather.

Note: The parking area and the lower portion of this hike are on land owned by Cochiti Pueblo. Pueblo officials have in the past been gracious about allowing hikers access, but you should be aware that the Pueblo may choose to restrict the public's use of its lands at any time.

RATING: Easy

ROUND TRIP HIKING DISTANCE: 5.5 miles.

APPROXIMATE ROUND TRIP HIKING TIME: 2½-3 hours.

ALTITUDE RANGE: Highest point, 6130 feet; lowest point, 5500 feet; cumulative uphill hiking, 630 feet.

SEASONAL CONSIDERATIONS: Too hot in mid-summer. Muddy in wet weather.

ROUND TRIP DRIVING: 55 miles; 1½ hours.

DRIVING DIRECTIONS: Take I-25 south toward Albuquerque. A bit more than 20 miles from Santa Fe, the highway begins the descent from the Santa Fe plateau. Halfway down the descent, turn right at Exit #264 onto NM #16, toward Cochiti. Drive 3.6 miles to a sign for La Bajada Village. Turn right and drive one mile, then turn right again onto a dirt road. After 1.5 miles, the road passes over the unimpressive Santa Fe River, then turns sharply left, toward the village center. Do not take this left turn. Leave the road at the bend and take the lesser road to the right. Drive about 50 feet and park in the open space on the right side of this road. You are at the base of La Bajada Mesa.

HIKING INSTRUCTIONS: While driving in toward La Bajada Village, you will have seen the switchbacks of an old roadbed climbing the mesa. You are parked on this old road, once the main link between Albuquerque and Santa Fe. For some motorists in early-model cars, the climb of La Bajada Hill was quite an adventure. An older friend of mine recalled for me a trip during his youth. His mother, fearing the switchback climb, removed him from the car. They walked up the road and rejoined his father in the car to continue the drive along the top of the mesa toward Santa Fe.

Following my friend's example, start walking up the road, turning periodically to look back at the view as you rise above the plain. In about half a mile, after several switchbacks, you will reach a "Y" intersection. Take the right fork (you will return on the other fork). As you near the top of the mesa, scan the vertical rock wall on your left occasionally. You may find the remains of old advertisements for accommodations and services in Santa Fe scratched or painted on the rocks.

Upon reaching the mesa top, take time to get your bearings. As it did for early travelers from the south, Tetilla Peak will serve as a convenient landmark. "Tetilla" means breast or nipple, and this pointed peak is easily identifiable almost due north ahead of you, under the telephone line, as you come up onto the mesa top. (See p. 120 for the Tetilla Peak hike.) Follow the road ruts heading toward Tetilla.

In about three quarters of a mile, just before reaching a power line, you will come to a crossroad. The tip of Tetilla Peak will be just visible behind a rise. You may choose to turn left here and return on the alternate road. This will shorten the hike by about 1.5 miles, but you will also miss some of the beautiful views. If you want to take the whole hike, then leave the road and climb the slight rise. Your course now runs cross-country over the trailless mesa top to the northwest. You may share the mesa top with grazing cattle. In the distance, a ridge from Tetilla extends in a westerly direction (to your left) to the end of the mesa. Head toward the western end of this ridge. After a little less than a mile, you will reach the mesa edge above the mouth of a canyon cutting into the mesa. Find a comfortable rock and take time out for a snack and scenery break. Look for horned larks, which are common on the mesa. Over the edge of the mesa, you will see the Jemez Mountains along the horizon far to your right. Closer in are Cochiti Lake and Dam. Just beyond the dam is Cochiti Pueblo. Toward your left is Sandia Mountain, near Albuquerque, and at the foot of the mesa is La Bajada Village.

The walk back is toward the south along the edge of the mesa. Enjoy the shadows of cloud patterns moving across the plain below. After about half a mile, you will have to turn in from the edge to get around a small side canyon. Otherwise, stay close enough to the edge to relish the view. This dropoff, wherever a road has been cut, has traditionally been called La Bajada (the descent). You may see a more modern form of descent, since hang gliders sometimes use the mesa edge along here as a stepping-off point.

Continue south until you spot the power line, a little over a mile from your snack spot. There is a power line tower at the edge where the road starts down. Take this branch of the old road down to the "Y" intersection where you turned off on your way up, and continue back down to your car.

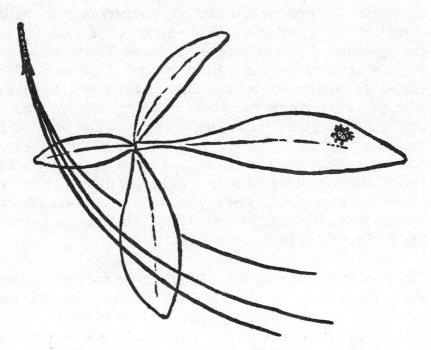

Large boulder

Tent Rocks

sling shot ponderosa

Start

N

Tent Rocks

½ mile

Forest rd. 266

to Cochiti

TENT ROCKS

by
Alan and Jenny Karp

U.S. GEOLOGICAL SURVEY MAP REQUIRED: Cañada - 7.5 minute series.

SALIENT FEATURES: Fascinating miniature canyon with unbelievable tuff rock formations, only 40 miles from Santa Fe. There are wildflowers in season. Spring or fall or early summer morning hours make this an idyllic short comfortable hike.

The canyon is very photogenic; even if you don't bring a camera, the banded striations, shadowed cliffs, and gravity-defiant rocks will be ever with you. You will probably want to explore the tent rocks near the road after you return to your car.

RATING: Easy.

ROUND TRIP HIKING DISTANCE: 2 miles.

APPROXIMATE ROUND TRIP HIKING TIME: 1½ hours.

ALTITUDE RANGE: Highest point, 6100 feet; lowest point, 5750 feet; cumulative uphill hiking, 350 feet.

SEASONAL CONSIDERATIONS: Not a winter hike if there has been heavy snowfall.

ROUND TRIP DRIVING: 80 miles; approximately 2 hours.

DRIVING DIRECTIONS: Take I-25 south toward Albuquerque and get off at the Cochiti exit #264. Take the right turn (west) off the exit ramp onto State Road #16. In about 8 miles you will come to a "T" intersection. Turn right here onto State Road #22 and follow this road for about 2.5 miles. Look for an intersection where you will take a sharp turn left (still State Road #22) toward Cochiti Pueblo. Stay on this road for 1.8 miles. To the right of the road you will see a water tower painted like an Indian drum and then a similar but narrower tower. After passing a sign, "←Cochiti Pueblo," you will come to an intersection where a gravel road comes in from the right. This road is marked, "266, Tent Rocks." Turn right onto this road. In about 3 miles you will pass a windmill on your left. After another 2 miles you will come to a well-used triangular driveway to the right. There is a small sign, "Parking," and a large sign, "Welcome to Tent Rocks." Turn right and park.

HIKING INSTRUCTIONS: Look for a wide trail that will take you to an information board protected by a roof. Here you will find descriptions and pictures of the area and a map. Your trail goes past this structure and, after some 50 yards, branches. Take the right branch. It continues straight ahead. Occasionally, the trail is marked by brown plastic stakes. Whenever you come to a trail junction or fork, take the right branch, toward the cliffs.

After about 7 minutes of hiking, your trail merges with a wash. Keep on going straight ahead, following the wash upstream. About 30 yards into the wash, you will pass a distinctive double-header "slingshot" ponderosa on your right. There is a large cairn next to this tree. The tree and the cairn are landmarks that you are on the right track. Continue up the wash which branches and then comes together again. In a few minutes, it will take you into an enchanting narrow canyon.

171

Mother Nature's imagination went wild in this stone wonderland. Over the ages, wind and water have sensuously carved out this inspiring miniature canyon, a micro Grand Canyon that envelopes and entices you with its cap rocks and volcanic tuff, ponderosa-lined trail and cheerful wildflowers. It gives you a very special spiritual feeling.

The arroyo funnels into this inner sanctuary. As you wind your way up the canyon, the soft curving walls provide you with meditative niches. The sky appears a deeper blue than imaginable and provides a dramatic backdrop for the still-forming tent rocks.

Approximately fifteen minutes into the hike, a tall ponderosa and a lone tent rock appear at the base of the left wall of the canyon. The wall bears petroglyphs depicting a serpent, handprints and other symbols.

The miniature canyon narrows into a stone hallway in which at several places you must scramble over rock steps. At one point you will need to crawl on hands and knees under a huge boulder. Some hikers may require a helping hand or a boost. The trail continues to wind, alternating between open and more narrow sections. You will finally arrive at a boulder in a fall of small rocks going up through a narrow passage. Access is difficult here and most hikers will make this the turn-around point of the hike.

For the hardy and more adventurous, a helping hand will be needed to scale the fallen boulder. If you scale it you will see a tall ponderosa stump on the left of the canyon. A trail starts here to your left paralleling the fallen ponderosa trunk. The trail ascends a razor-back ridge to the upper mesa several hundred yards away and some 300 feet above. The ascent is difficult on a steep trail with poor footing made slippery by loose gravel and sand. It may be scary for some. The vista from the mesa top will give a super northern New Mexico view; to the east is the familiar shape of Tetilla Peak above Cochiti Lake, to the north are the Sangre de

Cristo Mountains, and to the south is an interesting view of Sandia Peak.

On your return, after leaving the canyon, watch for the slingshot ponderosa. Thirty yards past this tree, the wash turns left. You go straight ahead, out of the wash, and back to your car.

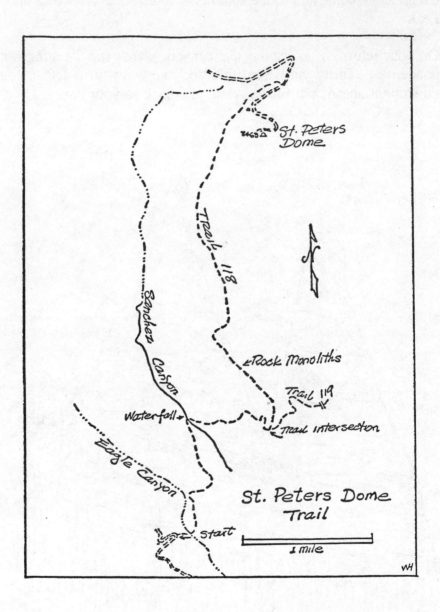

St. Peters Dome

Trail 118

Rock Monoliths

Trail 119

Sanchez Canyon

Waterfall

Trail intersection

Eagle Canyon

start

St. Peters Dome
Trail

1 mile

VH

174

ST. PETER'S DOME TRAIL

by
Kristin Eppler

U.S. GEOLOGICAL SURVEY MAPS REQUIRED: Cañada, Bland, Frijoles and Cochiti Dam - 7.5 minute series.

SALIENT FEATURES: Best western access trail to Dome Wilderness and Bandelier National Monument. Unusual volcanic formations, active waterfall, extensive views of the Sandias, Ortiz, San Pedros, Caja del Rio, Cochiti Dam, and Sangre de Cristos. This out and back hike gets little use except in deer and elk season; wear red clothing and leave dogs at home when the hunters are out.

RATING: Strenuous.

ROUND TRIP HIKING DISTANCE: 12 miles.

APPROXIMATE ROUND TRIP HIKING TIME: 7-8 hours.

ALTITUDE RANGE: Highest point, 8464 feet; lowest point, 6570 feet; cumulative uphill hiking, 2500 feet.

SEASONAL CONSIDERATIONS: Can be hiked year-round when access is open; high temperatures during summer.

ROUND TRIP DRIVING: 80 miles; 2 hours.

DRIVING DIRECTIONS: Take I-25 south toward Albuquerque. At Exit #264 turn right onto Highway #16 to a "T" junction with Highway #22. Turn right on #22 to Cochiti Village, beyond the Dam. Take your mileage at the Village. Continue for 2.7 miles past the golf course to Forest Road #289, which may be marked with a sign, "Dome Road." If there is no sign, you can identify the intersection by the Cochiti Stables on your left. Turn right on FR #289. You will cross a cattle guard with a sign warning that the road is unsuitable for passenger cars. This road is passable when dry; when wet or snow-covered, the road is unsuitable and treacherous for any vehicle. FR #289 is often closed during winter months. At 3.8 miles, the road crosses a shallow ford (Rio Chiquito). You may wish to check the depth during spring runoff. At 4.8 miles, you cross the Forest Boundary. At 6.2 miles, you will approach a climbing left turn. Look for signs, "Dome Wilderness→" and "Trail 118." Park your car at this corner.

HIKING INSTRUCTIONS: Thirty yards along the trail, there is a sign, "Dome Trail 118," followed by a sign referring to Bandelier National Monument, followed by another "Trail 118" sign. The trail descends steeply into Eagle Canyon. It crosses the canyon diagonally and climbs up on the opposite side, winding between and around huge boulders. After reaching the top, the trail levels out briefly, then starts to descend again, heading toward a rocky slope. When you come close to the rocks, your trail turns to the right. You will find a small sign, "118," on a tree to your right. The trail that, at this point, comes in from the left is the old trail, abandoned by the Forest Service, but still used by some hikers. Note this junction so you will know where to turn left on the return trip. Some 2 minutes later, you will go through a gate marked, "Dome Wilderness."

The trail continues in an easy climb and soon overlooks Sanchez Canyon. This area is noted for its massive volcanic outcroppings and is the home of many alligator junipers, easily identifed by their scaly bark. Your trail now swings to your left and descends into

Sanchez Canyon on a long gradual traverse to the Rito Sanchez and the Sanchez Falls. The trail crosses the stream just above the falls, turns sharply right and begins to climb. The best location to view the falls is about 100 yards past the stream crossing. An alligator juniper on your left marks an open space for viewing. There is (nonpotable) water in the Rito Sanchez almost every month of the year, and the falls are quite spectacular at times of heavy runoff.

The trail crosses a series of small arroyos and, a mile after the stream crossing, climbs out of the canyon. When you reach level ground, you will come to a trail junction. The trail that continues straight ahead goes to destinations inside Bandelier. Your trail goes off to the left and uphill. The junction may be marked by a signpost; if so, the sign referring to your trail says, "←FR 142 4." If the signs are gone, look for a cairn some 15 yards up on this trail. Continue climbing on a well-defined trail that traverses around to a point overlooking Picacho Canyon. The trail now roller-coasters along a gradual climb as it enters Picacho Canyon and soon you pass under a large rock outcropping that produces a small waterfall during spring runoff. During wet years this dripping spring falls on the trail and has been utilized as a welcome shower by overheated hikers.

Your trail now climbs through a conifer forest and continues under many interesting rock monoliths. At the base of Cerro Picacho the trail swings right and traverses along Cerro Picacho's eastern slope, coming out on a steep, rising ridge between Cerro Picacho and St. Peter's Dome. At the base of St. Peter's Dome your trail swings left and traverses the west slope of St. Peter's until it tops out in an abandoned picnic area and connects with St. Peter's Dome Forest Road #142. A half-mile climb up this road brings you to the top of St. Peter's Dome and a USFS lookout tower. There are views in every direction. You have now hiked approximately 6 miles and this is an excellent place for lunch (not a safe place during electrical storms, however). Return to your car the same way you hiked up.

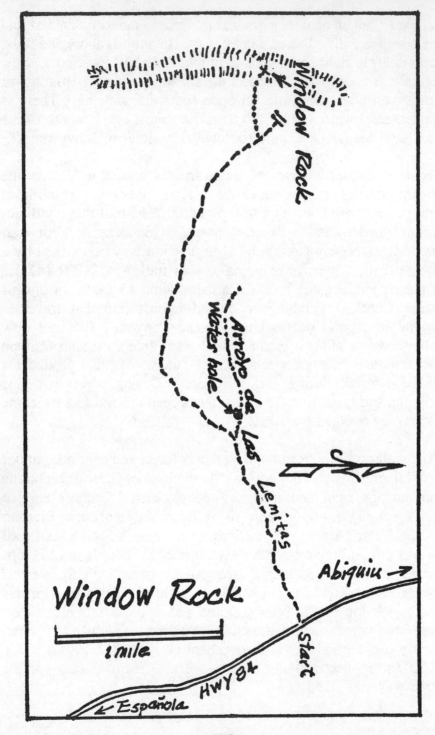

Window Rock

ⅼ mile

Window Rock

Arroyo de las Lemitas

Water hole

Abiquiu →

Start

HWY 84

← Española

178

WINDOW ROCK

by
Norbert Sperlich

U.S. GEOLOGICAL SURVEY MAPS REQUIRED: Chili and Medanales - 7.5 minute series. Most of the hike follows an unmarked, abandoned jeep trail. To find the trail on the topo maps (1953 edition), start with the Medanales map. Look for Highway #84 at the lower margin of the map. Follow the highway up for ¾ inch to where Arroyo de las Lemitas comes in from the left (west). This is the start of the hike. Follow the arroyo for ½ inch and you will see a "T" junction of jeep trails (indicated by broken lines). Follow the trail that goes up the arroyo and into the Chili topo map. There, the trail leaves the arroyo. It goes back into the Medanales map, where it comes close to Window Rock.

SALIENT FEATURES: Since the jeep trail you will hike on is not marked or maintained, this is a hike for experienced hikers only. Much of the terrain is sandy (look for animal tracks), but there are some rough and rocky spots as well. You will hike in a sandy arroyo, go up on a ridge through badlands, and come to a "window" or hole that has been weathered out of a dike (a rock wall formed by igneous rocks). There are great views from Window Rock and along the way. You are in the piñon-juniper belt, and you will also encounter cottonwoods, tamarisk, mountain mahogany, and a stand of ponderosa pines.

RATING: Moderate.

ROUND TRIP HIKING DISTANCE: About 8 miles.

APPROXIMATE ROUND TRIP HIKING TIME: 5 hours.

ALTITUDE RANGE: Highest point, 6463 feet; lowest point, 5800 feet; cumulative uphill hiking, about 1000 feet.

SEASONAL CONSIDERATIONS: All seasons, but not recommended in hot weather. If you go in summer, take extra water.

ROUND TRIP DRIVING: 70 miles; 1½ hours or more.

DRIVING DIRECTIONS: Take US #84/285 northbound from Santa Fe to Española. At the first signal light in Española, turn left and cross the Rio Grande. At the next light, turn right. Get in the left lane as you approach the third light and turn left. You are still on US #84/285. About 6 miles north of Española, Route #285 separates from Route #84. Keep going straight on Route #84. Look for the green mile posts on the right side of the road. Slow down when you pass mile post 200. About 0.1/mile after this post look for a grey, barn-like building (made from corrugated sheet metal) on your right. Some 40 yards past this building, a power line crosses the highway, and a paved private driveway goes off to the right. Go just past this driveway and park your car on the side of the highway.

HIKING INSTRUCTIONS: Cross the highway. On the west side of the highway is a fence marked "Property Boundary, National Forest." Cross the fence and go down into a sandy arroyo which comes in from the west. Follow the car tracks that run parallel to the arroyo along its right (north) side. If the tracks are gone, follow the arroyo, staying on its right side. Disregard a jeep trail that goes off to the right. Some 7 minutes or so into the hike, you should see a freestanding, orange-brown rock ahead of you on the right side of the arroyo. In another 5 minutes or so you will be close to this rock. In front of the rock is a rectangular, green water tank and a well. The car tracks (your "trail") pass the tank on the left and go in and out of the arroyo. There are cotton-woods, elm trees, and tamarisks along your way, and sandy hills with piñon and juniper along the sides of the arroyo. Here and there, you will encounter light grey rocks, formed by sand particles that have been cemented together. Often, the surface of these rocks is covered with balls or nodules consisting of cemented sand. These balls come in different sizes: peppercorns, peas, tennis balls, and larger.

A little over a mile into the hike (it seems longer because of the sandy terrain) the arroyo starts to narrow down. Just where it makes a turn to the right, look for a jeep trail that goes out of the arroyo and uphill on your left. This is your trail to Window Rock.

(Note: If you have 20 minutes extra time, you might want to continue in the arroyo for a little side trip. Remember the place where the jeep trail climbs out of the arroyo. After passing this spot, follow the arroyo, which turns to the right. On your right, the arroyo is bordered by walls of compacted sand. Scratched into the sand are inscriptions such as LA LOCA PARTY, MARIJUA-NA, LU ANN. In a few minutes, you will come to a water hole. Beyond the water hole, the terrain becomes rocky and steep. The water hole is a great place for a stop. Many birds come here to drink, and you will hear their songs in the nearby trees. Go back to where the jeep trail leaves the arroyo, now on your right.)

The trail climbs to the top of a ridge and follows the ridge line. Here and there, the trail is blocked by mounds of dirt. You are surrounded by badlands dotted with juniper bushes and mountain mahogany. There are more of the grey sandstone formations sculpted by the elements. About 20 minutes after leaving the arroyo, you come to a high point on the ridge, with splendid views in all directions. Ahead of you are the Jemez Mountains; to the east you will see the Sangre de Cristo Range, with the flat-topped Black Mesa in the foreground. As you continue your hike, the ridge widens and levels out. Soon, it narrows again and the trail goes steeply uphill. Here, the ground is covered with loose rocks, and the going is rough until you reach level ground again. Ahead of you, to the left, you will see a ridge that is crested by a dark rock wall, sticking out like a spine.

Look for a hole in the rocks. That's Window Rock! For about three quarters of a mile, the jeep trail goes gently downhill, taking you to a flat, treeless area. This is a reservoir where water collects after heavy rains. Window Rock is to your left. Here you leave the jeep trail and go toward Window Rock. Just below the ridge, there is a sandy bank with tall ponderosa pines. This is a great spot for a break before ascending the ridge.

Look for a drainage coming down to the left of Window Rock. Climb up on the rock-strewn slope to the left of this drainage. As you near the top of the ridge, bear to the right and onto a trail leading to the other side of the dike and to the window. You can take great pictures looking through the window toward the east, especially if you have a wide-angle lens. Caution should be taken if you climb up on the dike. It is only 6 feet wide. Do not attempt to cross over the top of the window. Enjoy the views and the solitude, then return the way you came.

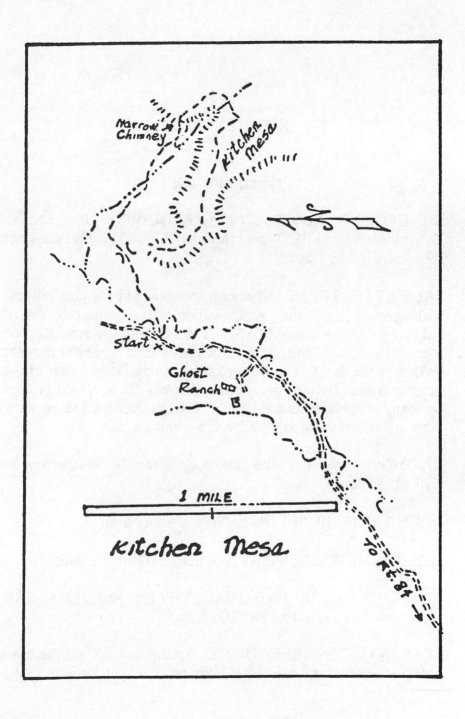

Narrow
Chimney

Kitchen
mesa

Start x

Ghost
Ranch

1 MILE

Kitchen Mesa

To Rt. 84

KITCHEN MESA

by
Norma McCallan

U.S. GEOLOGICAL SURVEY MAP REQUIRED: Ghost Ranch - 7.5 minute series - 1953, photorevised 1979. This trail does not show on the topo map.

SALIENT FEATURES: All-season access and hiking possibilities, striking vistas, interesting geological features, the best display of red rock in northern New Mexico. The origin of the name Kitchen Mesa is unknown. The director of Ghost Ranch suggested it might be due to the fact that it overlooks the dining/kitchen area of the ranch. Owned by the Presbyterian Church, Ghost Ranch is used by many organizations and groups for conferences and retreats. Staff are friendly and knowledgeable about the area.

RATING: Easy, but with one rock scramble which may be difficult for some.

ROUND TRIP HIKING DISTANCE: About 5 miles.

APPROXIMATE ROUND TRIP HIKING TIME: 2½ hours.

ALTITUDE RANGE: Highest point, 7077 feet; lowest point, 6500 feet; cumulative uphill hiking, 600 feet.

SEASONAL CONSIDERATIONS: Spring and fall are the most pleasant. Winter might be ok if there has not been a recent heavy snowfall or rainstorm in the area. Summer will be hot; try to get an early start in the cool of the morning.

ROUND TRIP DRIVING: 122 miles; approximately 2 hours 45 minutes.

DRIVING DIRECTIONS: From the plaza, drive north on Washington Avenue, left on Paseo de Peralta, and right on Old Taos Highway to US #84/285, continuing north to Española (approximately 23.5 miles). At the first traffic light in Española turn left and cross the Rio Grande. At the next light, turn right and continue on Route #84/285. Get into the left lane as you approach the third light. Turn left, still on Route #84/285. Stay on Route #84 (straight ahead) where Routes #84 and #285 separate about 6 miles north of Española. Continue north through the village of Abiquiu. When you come to the Abiquiu Dam turnoff (Hwy #96), note your odometer reading. Continue north on US #84 for about 6 miles where you will see, on the right, a wooden sign for Ghost Ranch. Turn here and drive up the dirt road. Note the historic-looking log cabin on the right; it was actually built for the set of the movie, "City Slickers." At 1.1 miles the road forks; stay left, and stop at the Ghost Ranch Office to sign in for your hike. The office is generally open 8-5 everyday; a small library and museum next door has more restricted hours. Continue up this road, turning left 0.2/mile further, toward "Teepee Village" and "Trails to Kitchen Mesa & Box Canyon." After another 0.3/mile, you will reach a parking area with a sign which says "No vehicles allowed beyond this point." Park here. There is a water faucet on the right to fill your canteens.

HIKING INSTRUCTIONS: Follow the dirt road a few yards down a short hill and you will see a sign pointing right for Kitchen Mesa. Follow the trail across a shallow stream and up the far bank. You will start to see faded blue-painted coffee cans nailed upside down on small posts; these markers continue intermittently the whole length of the trail. The trail follows the river bank a short distance, then joins an old dirt road going up the hill to the right, through the deep red Chinle formation soils of the valley floor. After 5 to 10 minutes of walking, the trail takes you up to the top of a low, but steep, ridge. At the top you will see a well-trodden shortcut going downhill in front of you, but the actual trail (which is less steep) goes left along the ridge line a few yards before heading down. You can now see, to your right, the small box canyon stretching southeast, which the trail follows, ascending by degrees to the mesa top at the far end.

After meandering along the base of some wonderfully sculpted Entrada sandstone cliffs, the trail crosses an arroyo and starts going up the rocky talus slope of the canyon wall. The trail is steep from here to the top, so proceed slowly and watch your footing. The loose clay soils can be quite difficult to cross when muddy. About halfway up, you will begin having to traverse around or over large boulders. There are several dead-end paths branching off to the right of the main trail in this section, so keep your eye out for the blue coffee cans and a few faded arrows painted on the rocks which delineate the actual trail.

Just before you reach the top, you will find yourself directly in front of a sheer cliff. Look to the left and you will see a slot in the rocks. You will need to scramble up this narrow passage. The first part is the most difficult. There are adequate foot and hand holds if you look around for them; however, you will need to hoist a small child or your dog up the steepest section, and some adults may want help from their hiking companions. It may not be possible to get very heavy dogs up this vertical rock; the author was unable to hoist her 125-pound Rottweiler up here, even with the help of a friend.

When you reach the top, note carefully where the passage is, since the slot is not easy to see from the top.

The trail now veers right, crosses an arroyo, and goes steeply up on easily ascended sandstone ledges to the top of the mesa. The trail markers are farther apart here, but visible if you look for them. Once up, you can easily see the trail heading north, to your right, along a flat peninsula to the chalky white, lunar landscape at its end. This porous, hollow-sounding substance is called the Todilto Formation and is gypsum deposited by a lake that evaporated millions of years ago. Roam around this point, and enjoy the magnificent views, but don't get too close to the edge since the gypsum is crumbly and the cliffs below it are sheer and steep.

Walk back a few hundred yards to the beginning of the vegetation, find a comfortable rock outcropping under a wind-sculpted juniper, take out your picnic lunch, and feast your senses. All is silence, sky, and magnificent rock formations. Ghost Ranch, surrounded by green fields, sits right under the cliffs. The ridge immediately to the north of it is Mesa Montosa, and the further ridge to the northwest is Mesa de los Viejos (see page 188 for the Rim Vista/ Salazar Trail hike). El Vado Lake spreads out to the west, and Cerro Pedernal (see page 199 for the Cerro Pedernal hike) is the prominent flat-topped peak on the southwest horizon. The multi-colored bluffs all around you expose geologic history, from the reddish purple Chinle Formation muds at the base to the tree-topped Dakota sandstone at the highest points. At your feet may be patches of cryptogamic soils, a crusted brown substance made up of mosses and lichens which take many years to form and are easily destroyed. Try not to step on them. The destruction of cryptogams is the most significant factor in the erosion of desert soils. You may see the grey-green leaves and small white trumpet-shaped flowers of Bigelow's sand abronia, or tufted sand verbena, a rare plant which grows only on Todilto gypsum soils.

Return the way you came. Some hikers find the descent difficult because they feel more exposed and footing is more precarious; in any case, proceed very slowly, and always with great care. Take time to enjoy the rich hues of the twisted juniper stumps as you return along the ridge, and, when descending the trail back down the canyon, look for a few stately Douglas firs nestled in the coolest, shadiest nooks of the rocky walls. Don't forget to sign out at the Ghost Ranch Office.

(Note: If you want to spend more time hiking in the area, you can take the short well-marked trail to Box Canyon, which starts at the same trailhead. Follow the signs along the streambed to a picturesque box canyon with steep walls and lush vegetation, whose subdued lighting reminds one of a mysterious grotto.

Ghost Ranch also provides a written description, available at the office for 25 cents, of the short Chimney Rock Trail, just north of the Ranch, with much useful geological information.

Two miles north of Ghost Ranch on the paved highway is the Ghost Ranch Living Museum. Run by the Carson National Forest, this museum, with its many wild animal exhibits and descriptions of the area, is also worth a visit.)

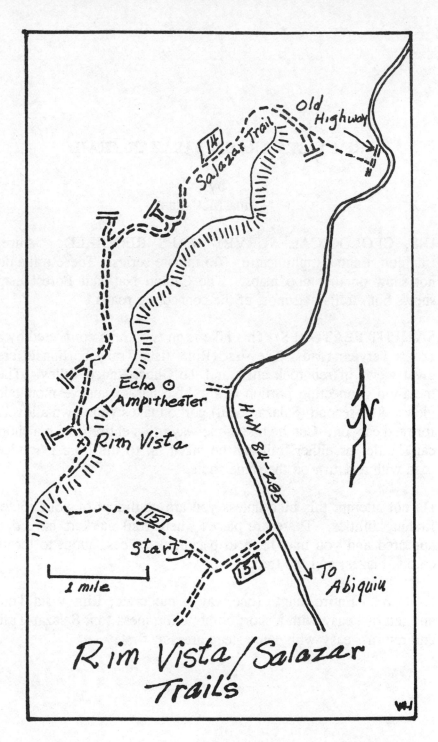

Old Highway

14

Salazar Trail

Echo ⊙ Ampitheater

× Rim Vista

Hwy 84-285

15

start →

151

To Abiquiu

1 mile

Rim Vista/Salazar Trails

RIM VISTA TRAIL - SALAZAR TRAIL

by
Norma McCallan

U.S. GEOLOGICAL SURVEY MAPS REQUIRED: Alire, Canjilon, Echo Amphitheatre - 7.5 minute series. These trails do not show on the topo maps. The Carson National Forest map shows both trails and most of the connecting roads.

SALIENT FEATURES: This hike is on two trails connected by a Forest Service road. The first (Rim Vista Trail) portion offers great views of red rock cliffs and the Ghost Ranch valley. The mesa-top connecting portion of the hike has expansive mountain views. The second (Salazar Trail) portion takes you down a lovely forested canyon. Can be hiked one-way in its entirety with a short car shuttle, or either trail can be hiked up to the Forest Service road with a return on the same route.

Do not attempt this hike unless you are confident of your route-finding abilities. There are places where trail markers have disappeared and you may have to backtrack or cast about to locate cairns, blazes, and the trail.

RATING: Entire length (one way) - moderate; Rim Vista Trail and return - easy with a short climb to the mesa top; Salazar Trail and return - easy with some steep areas at first.

ROUND TRIP HIKING DISTANCE: About 7.5 miles entire length (one way); Rim Vista Trail and return, about 4.5 miles round trip; Salazar Trail and return, about 5 miles round trip.

APPROXIMATE ROUND TRIP HIKING TIME: Entire length (one way), 5 hours; Rim Vista Trail and return, 2½ hours; Salazar Trail and return, 3 hours.

ALTITUDE RANGE: Highest point, 7900 feet; lowest point, 6200 feet; cumulative uphill hiking, 1700 feet.

SEASONAL CONSIDERATIONS: Best in spring or fall. Summer is very hot. In winter there may be snow on the mesa top and on the Salazar Trail. After heavy rains or in early spring during snowmelt, the dirt road into the Rim Vista Trailhead could be impassable.

ROUND TRIP DRIVING: Approximately 130 miles to Rim Vista Trailhead, 140 miles to Salazar Trailhead; 3-3½ hours.

DRIVING DIRECTIONS: From the plaza, drive north on Washington Avenue, left on Paseo de Peralta, and right on Old Taos Highway to US #84/285, continuing north to Española (approximately 23.5 miles). At the first traffic light in Española turn left and cross the Rio Grande. At the next light, turn right and continue on Route #84/285. Get into the left lane as you approach the third light. Turn left, still on Route #84/285. Stay on Route #84 (straight ahead) where Routes #84 and #285 separate about 6 miles north of Española. Continue north past the Abiquiu Dam turnoff (Hwy #96); you will start to see the striking red sandstone cliffs ahead which are the setting of the hike. Two miles after you pass the dirt road to Ghost Ranch, you will pass the Ghost Ranch Living Museum. Slow down; in one mile you will see a small BLM sign on the right pointing to Forest Road #151 to Rio Chama on the left.

If you will be hiking one way on the entire hike, note Forest Road #151, but continue driving north on Highway #84 past the Echo Amphitheatre Campground. At 5.1 miles beyond the FR #151 turnoff, immediately after a long guardrail on the left, you will see on the left, several yards off the road, a small shrine in the rocks. Although no road is visible, turn left at the end of the guardrail, and you will see a section of the old highway (now a dirt track) and a sign, "Virgin Maria," by the shrine. Turn left again immediately and go about 0.2/mile down the old highway to a Forest Service sign on the right for Trail #14, the Salazar Trail. Park in the grass. This is the trailhead for the Salazar Trail. If you reach an old bridge, you have gone too far.

If you are hiking the entire distance one-way, leave one car here and return in a second car on Highway #84 to the earlier turnoff to Forest Road #151. Turn right onto FR #151 and go 0.7/mile. Here at the top of a hill you will see a narrow dirt road going right, signed, "Trail 151 - Rim Vista 2.3 miles." Follow this road and, where it forks, stay right. In 0.3/mile you will reach the end of the road and the trailhead for both the Rim Vista Trail #15 and the one-way hike. Park here.

HIKING INSTRUCTIONS: Proceed up the well-trodden trail, which slowly wends its way uphill toward the cliff face to the north, passing through piñon-juniper forest with lots of Indian paintbrush, Perky Sue, and blue penstemon. In about 15 minutes, you will see the first blue diamond trail sign nailed to a piñon on the right. These blue diamond markers continue the entire length of the hike. Shortly before you reach the cliffs, at a partial clearing in the heavy piñon-juniper forest, the trail makes a sharp right. The trail is fainter here and you may fear you have lost the trail, but look to the right and you will see a blue diamond marker ahead as well as a blaze in a tall piñon near the turn. Just before the trail makes a sharp left to go up the cliffs, you will pass a large rock. This is a nice shady spot for a rest before ascending in the full sun.

The trail is now steep but well-graded. Almost immediately you will be rewarded by great views of Abiquiu Lake and the whole Ghost Ranch valley. Near the top, where you pass a small stone embankment, the trail once made a sharp left then angled gently up to the top. A fallen tree now obstructs this, and the Forest Service has marked with blue diamonds a shorter but steeper route to the right.

Once on the top, veer right for a few steps and you will reach a dirt road with a large brown sign facing away from you which says, "Carson National Forest Rim Vista Overlooking Ghost Ranch and Abiquiu Dam - 2.3 miles to FS Rd 151" (which of course is where you have come from). Find a comfortable seat on the rocks at the edge of the cliffs and feast your eyes on the magnificent vista: Pedernal and Chicoma Peaks are prominent to the south-west, Highway #84 snakes south, the red rock cliffs surrounding Ghost Ranch are to the southeast, and beyond them in the far distance are the snowy peaks of the Sangre de Cristos. Peace and solitude reign, broken only by the caws of the ravens cruising in the thermals and, far below, an occasional car on the highway. If your destination is Rim Vista, you have reached it, and you can simply return the way you came.

If you are hiking the entire one-way trip, you now head north on the dirt road, avoiding a dirt track to the left. In a few yards you will come to a "T" intersection. The Forest Service sign facing away from you on the right says "Road 131 - South Rim 3 miles further and Rim Vista, 131A, left." Turn right and continue to follow the blue diamonds. Now you are hiking on a high, open, sagebrush-covered plateau called Mesa de los Viejos (Old Ones' Mesa). In the distance is the (often) snowy ridge of the Canjilon Peaks and, further still, the high peaks at the southern end of the South San Juans. The dirt road heads roughly north; after rain or snow it can be quite muddy and you may share it with cows. Soon you will see a white barn to the left, which stays prominent for a long time. You will pass a small Forest Service sign (again facing away) indicating you are on Route #131 (this sign was down in the summer of 1994). Stay straight here where a dirt track comes in from the left. Soon you will cross a cattleguard and briefly find yourself back in piñon-juniper forest.

At the point where the dirt road starts to veer left, look for a blue diamond marker on a small piñon to the right and a brown sign noting 131TG, Trail #14, with an arrow pointing right. Turn right here and follow this faint track east. Happily, the blue diamonds continue to mark your way. Along this section, the trail stays just to the left of a narrow band of forest which follows along the edge of the cliffs. You can walk out to the edge at almost any point to take a break while you enjoy the views and watch the ravens play.

After about a mile, you will come to another "T" intersection with a sign indicating Trail #14 to the right and a blue diamond just ahead on your right. Go right on a dirt road which circles northeast, and in another quarter of a mile you will reach a brown sign noting "Trail Ahead." Ignore the ruts to the right. You will soon come upon a muddy cow pond. Here at this pond is where you reach the Salazar Trail.

Keep to the left around the pond. You will see a trail sign right after the pond and a series of large cairns which mark the trail as it moves down the floor of an emerging canyon. In less than half a mile, the trail leaves the canyon floor and proceeds along a bench on the south side of the canyon. The vegetation is quite different here from that on the mesa top or the Rim Vista Trail; you are walking amidst stately ponderosa pines and scrub oaks, and the temperature is 5-10 degrees cooler.

In another half mile or more, the trail becomes an old, unused, very rocky dirt road and the side canyon you have been following comes out into the main canyon. The road makes a sharp right to follow the main canyon south. In about a quarter of a mile from the right turn, you will pass a cairn on your left, then in a few

194

more yards come to a cairn on your right, just where the road is becoming less steep and rocky and more grassy. There may be a blue diamond on a tree on the right above the cairn. Here, the trail leaves the road and turns left into the woods. (If you are using the Forest Service map, you will note that only the trail, and not this old road, is shown.) If you look to the left you can spot several more cairns among the trees. Follow the faint but discernible trail as it heads slowly down toward the canyon floor, then more steeply into an arroyo at the bottom. After crossing the arroyo and going up its steep bank, the trail veers right across a smaller arroyo. It then heads south through an open, sagebrush-covered meadow and in no time at all arrives at the old highway where you parked your first car.

If you wish to hike only the Salazar Trail portion of this hike, just reverse the directions from the car at the trailhead for Trail #14 to the muddy cow pond, and return to your car by the same route.

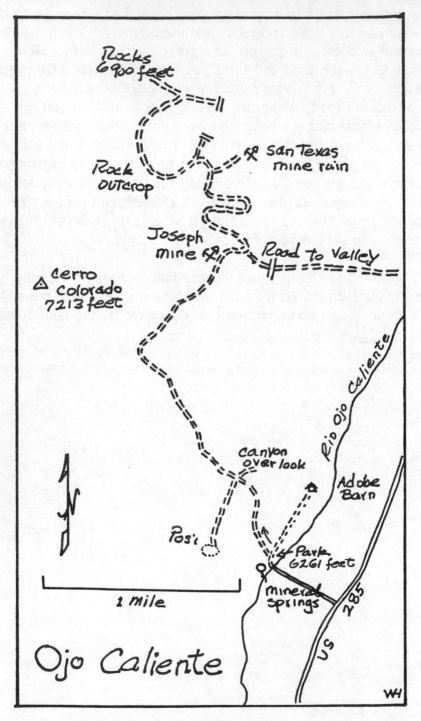

Rocks
6900 feet

Rock
outcrop

San Texas
mine ruin

Joseph
mine

Road to Valley

cerro
colorado
7213 feet

canyon
overlook

Rio Ojo Caliente

Adobe
Barn

Posi

Park
6261 feet

mineral
Springs

US 285

1 Mile

Ojo Caliente

WH

OJO CALIENTE

by
Norrine Sanders

U.S. GEOLOGICAL SURVEY MAP REQUIRED: Ojo Caliente - 7.5 minute series - 1953.

SALIENT FEATURES: National and State Historic Site. Historic adobe church, round adobe barn, ancient pueblo site (Pos'i), mica mine sites, tremendous views. Horseback riding and the Ojo Caliente Mineral Springs (five hot volcanic springs) also make the area worth a visit.

RATING: Easy to moderate.

ROUND TRIP HIKING DISTANCE: 3-6 miles.

APPROXIMATE ROUND TRIP HIKING TIME: 1½-4 hours.

ALTITUDE RANGE: Highest point, 6900 feet; lowest point, 6200 feet; cumulative uphill hiking, 700 feet.

SEASONAL CONSIDERATIONS: All seasons, but not recommended in very hot weather. Hikers are advised to check with the Department of Game and Fish for hunting regulations in the area during the fall; the hike area is on BLM land.

ROUND TRIP DRIVING: 100 miles; 2 hours.

197

DRIVING DIRECTIONS: Take Route #84/285 northbound from Santa Fe to Española. At the first traffic light in Española turn left and cross the Rio Grande. At the next light, turn right and continue on Route #84/285. Get into the left lane as you approach the third light. Turn left, still on Route #84/285, and drive north 6.3 miles to where Route #285 separates from Route #84. Take the right turn here. Continue north on #285 about 17 miles to the village of Ojo Caliente. The Ojo Caliente Post Office is on your left; just past it is the left turn to the mineral springs. Drive toward the springs, making a right turn at a row of cottages. Drive through the open gate and park in the large parking area under the cottonwood trees. The road ahead of you goes to the Round Barn, about a quarter-mile away and worth a visit.

HIKING INSTRUCTIONS: The hike starts up the steep hill just to the west of and across from the parking area. The hike follows old mining roads on BLM land. Five minutes into the hike, there is a road on the left which goes to the water tower above the hot springs resort; you continue on the main road. In another ten minutes or so, a road going to the left will take you to the Pos'i ruin, a huge circle of scattered stones and many pottery shards; you can explore the ruin as a side trip. A second side trip is on the faint road opposite the road to the ruin, which leads to a pictur-esque canyon with a steep drop to the Ojo Caliente valley.

By following the main road for another 30 minutes or so (about 1.5 miles from the beginning of the hike), you will reach the Joseph Mica Mine on the left. There is a narrow trail over to the three mine shafts, one of which is large enough to enter. The mine site is a good place for a break and some exploring to the top of the hill above the mine. Mica mines were operated commercially until the 1960s.

By following the road around the Joseph Mica Mine (ignore the road to the right that goes down into the valley) up the hill and then straight ahead down the hill on a long switchback, you will reach a second mine, on the left at the bottom of the canyon. This second mine is propped up with wooden beams and is not safe to enter. Continue to follow the road up the opposite side of the canyon. In about 10 minutes, there will be another road on the right. This road will take you to even more mining activity (mostly broken-down ramps) and makes an interesting exploratory side trip that adds about 15 minutes to your hike. The main hiking road turns left. In another 5 minutes, the road divides again, with a dead-end road to the right. Take the left fork, which continues up rather steeply. In about 10 more minutes, you will reach an outcrop of stone on the left which makes a good spot for lunch and a turn-around point of the hike. You have now hiked about 2.5 miles.

You may want to extend the hike by another mile by following the road up to an even more spectacular outcrop about half a mile from the first. There is a very steep pitch up to these rocks but the views of the high mountains to the north and east are excellent.

Return by the same route. At the bottom of the steep pitch, the main road turns right. It is an easy mistake to go straight ahead on a faint road here.

A mineral bath makes a nice finish to this hike.

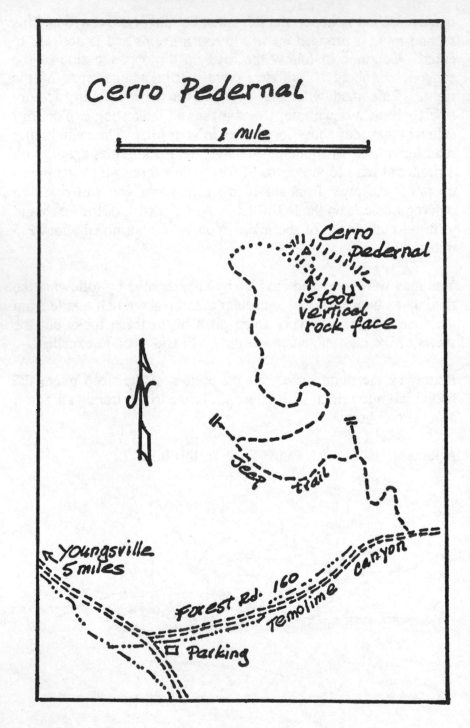

Cerro Pedernal

1 mile

Cerro Pedernal

15 foot vertical rock face

Jeep Trail

Youngsville 5 miles

Forest Rd. 160

Temolime Canyon

□ Parking

CERRO PEDERNAL

by
John Muchmore and Norbert Sperlich

U.S. GEOLOGICAL SURVEY MAPS REQUIRED: Youngsville and Cañones - 7.5 minute series.

SALIENT FEATURES: Cerro Pedernal is a landmark well known throughout north-central New Mexico. Its truncated pyramid shape is visible from Taos to Cuba and from Chama to Española. The mountain has appeared in works by famous (and less well-known) American artists. From its summit, you will enjoy sweeping views in all directions.

Cerro Pedernal is Spanish for "Flint Mountain." Flint (a variety of quartz) can be found on the lower slopes of the mountain at about 8500 feet. For more than 10,000 years, Indians have used the flint from Cerro Pedernal to make arrowheads and tools.

Much of the hike is on unmarked jeep trails; the last part is steep and trailless. This hike is not suitable for inexperienced hikers and not recommended for solo hiking. While hiking on the jeep trails, make sure that you don't miss a turnoff. Topo maps and compass are essential for orientation in case you lose your bearing. The last part of the hike is steep and rocky, and can be dangerous unless you are confident of your ability to climb up and down a vertical 15-foot rock face (dogs will not be able to negotiate the climb to the summit). Sturdy boots with good traction are required. This is dry country, so carry sufficient water and be prepared for wind, cold, and rain.

RATING: Moderate in miles, strenuous due to steep climbs.

ROUND TRIP HIKING DISTANCE: Approximately 9 miles.

APPROXIMATE ROUND TRIP HIKING TIME: 6-7 hours, including ample time for stops.

ALTITUDE RANGE: Highest point, 9862 feet; lowest point, 8000 feet; cumulative uphill hiking, 1862 feet.

SEASONAL CONSIDERATIONS: Not safe when snow hides the jeep trails. The best time to visit is in the spring, fall, and early winter. A favorite area for elk and deer hunters.

ROUND TRIP DRIVING: 146 miles; approximately 3½ hours.

DRIVING DIRECTIONS: Take Route #84/285 northbound from Santa Fe to Española. At the first traffic light in Española turn left and cross the Rio Grande. At the next light, turn right and continue on Route #84/285. Get into the left lane as you approach the third light. Turn left, still on Route #84/285. Stay on Route #84 (straight ahead) where Routes #84 and #285 separate about 6 miles north of Española. Continue north through the village of Abiquiu until you reach the Abiquiu Dam turnoff. There, turn left on Highway #96. Take your mileage at this intersection. Continue approximately 11 miles to the outskirts of Youngsville. As you approach a "Youngsville" sign, look for a gravel road that comes in on your left. This is Forest Road #100 (Rito Encino Road). Turn left onto the gravel road and follow this road for about 5.5 miles, until you see a dirt road branch off to the left. Turn left onto this road and park your car in the meadow immediately after the turnoff. You are now on Forest Road #160, the Temolime Canyon jeep road. The road is not marked at the turnoff.

However, a sign "160" appears some 100 yards along the road. The Temolime Canyon road is on the Youngsville and Cañones topo maps.

HIKING INSTRUCTIONS: Follow Forest Road #160 up Temolime Canyon for about 1 mile (20 minutes or more) to a fork in the road. Forest Road #160 continues straight ahead, but you take the jeep road that goes to the left (north). (This road appears on the topo maps as a broken line. On the Cañones map, look for the second "m" in the word "Temolime." That is where the road starts.) Ignore an abandoned logging road that branches right. In a few minutes, you will cross a drainage where the road turns to the left and starts climbing. Soon, the road turns to the right (north) again, and it appears to head toward the eastern end of the Pedernal summit ridge. Some 5 minutes after crossing the drainage, you may notice a block of flint to your right, with a "2" spray-painted on it. All around, and especially to the left of the road, are pieces of flint on the ground.

In a few more minutes, you will come to a fork in the road. The fork might be marked by a cairn on the left. The road straight ahead (not shown on the topo map) appears to go toward the summit, but you take the road that goes off to the LEFT, in a westerly direction. Look at your watch. About 15 minutes after taking the left fork, as you are going uphill, you will notice a drainage on your left, where Gambel oaks are growing. Just before your road is about to cross the drainage and make a turn to the left, look to your right. A road comes in sharply behind you on the right, and there might be a cairn marking this intersection.

Take the road that comes in from the right. It is not on the Youngsville topo map, but its approximate location is shown on the sketch map. At first, you will climb steeply in an easterly direction. Then the road turns north, toward the summit ridge. It crosses a drainage and starts climbing again, turning to the left, away from the summit. This is obviously not the shortest way to

203

get to the top! After briefly heading south, the road turns right to almost level ground. In a few minutes, you will come to the first of a series of meadows. From the last intersection you have now hiked some 25 minutes or more.

For a while, the road heads toward the center of the summit ridge, then turns left and runs parallel to the ridge. Foiled again! In the meadows, the jeep tracks may not be highly visible. When you emerge into a meadow, <u>mark your entrance</u>; it is easy to get lost on the way down! Follow the jeep tracks past the western end of the summit ridge to a level spot between two pine trees. You have now hiked 40 minutes or more since the last intersection. Ahead of you, the terrain starts to descend, opening up splendid vistas over valleys, mesas, and mountain ranges. Take a break and enjoy the views.

It will take another hour or so of strenuous hiking to reach the summit. Look to your right. A talus slope, studded with scrub oak and piñon, rises up to the end of the basalt ridge that forms the summit. There is no trail here. Head up toward the narrow end of the ridge, avoiding scrub oaks and loose rocks as best you can. When you reach the vertical basalt cliffs, go to the right and follow a faint trail that runs along the base of the cliffs. After about 150 yards (some 10 minutes of hiking) the trail passes between the cliff wall on the left and a large juniper tree on the right. (If you come to a cave in the rocks on your left, you have gone too far. Go back and look for the juniper tree.) Follow the trail 10 yards past the juniper tree. Stop and look. To the right of the trail, there might be a cairn, and to your left, leaning against the rock wall, might be a log pole. The cliff on your left is somewhat broken up, providing hand and foot holds. This is the place to climb up, or to call it a day if it looks too scary to you. The first 15 feet are nearly vertical, but then you will come to a rough trail that goes up to your right, leading to the top of the ridge. Watch for loose rocks! When you come to the flat top, look for cairns. They will tell you where to start your descent on the way back. Any other way down is dangerous. Continue left on the ridge to its western end. This is the highest point of Pedernal.

After you have enjoyed the views, you might want to go to the other end of the ridge, where the views are toward the east. Then find the cairn that marks the descent, and start your way down to the base of the cliffs. Once there, you will be tempted to head straight down to the jeep trail in the meadow below. However, to stay out of harm's way (and avoid loose rocks on a very steep slope) return to the meadow the same way you came up. Find the jeep road and retrace your route back to your car.

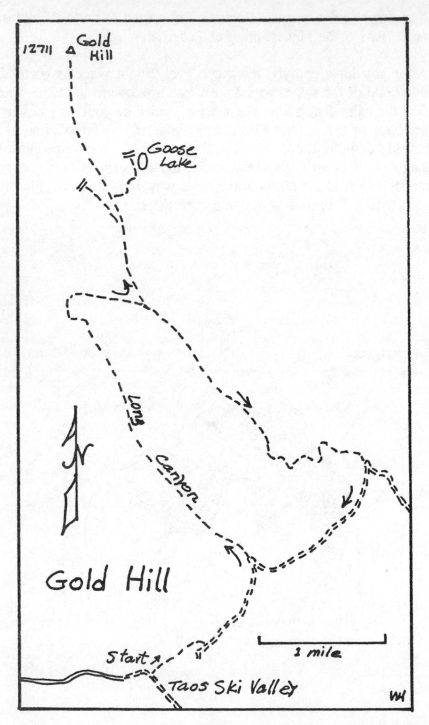

12711 △ Gold Hill

Goose Lake

Long Canyon

Gold Hill

Start

1 mile

Taos Ski Valley

WH

GOLD HILL

by
John Jasper

U.S. GEOLOGICAL SURVEY MAPS REQUIRED: Wheeler Peak and Red River - 7.5 minute series. Also recommended is the US Forest Service Map of the Carson National Forest.

SALIENT FEATURES: Spectacular views of highest peaks, including Wheeler; alpine flowers in summer and golden aspen in fall. An interesting loop trip via Long Canyon and Gold Hill Trails above Taos.

RATING: Strenuous.

ROUND TRIP HIKING DISTANCE: 10 miles.

APPROXIMATE ROUND TRIP HIKING TIME: 6+ hours.

ALTITUDE RANGE: Highest point, 12,711 feet; lowest point, 9300 feet; cumulative uphill hiking, 3411 feet.

SEASONAL CONSIDERATIONS: Not a winter hike. Parts of the trail may be snow-covered through June, and snowfall comes early in the autumn this far north and this high. Get an early start, since you do not want to be above timberline during summer's afternoon thunderstorms.

ROUND TRIP DRIVING: 184 miles; approximately 4½ hours.

DRIVING DIRECTIONS: From Santa Fe, take US #84/285 northbound to Española. Do not take the left turn when #84 turns, but continue straight through Española on SR #68 to Taos. Travel north through Taos, continuing north on SR #68 for about 4 miles from the center of Taos to the junction with SR #150. Turn right onto SR #150 and drive to the Taos Ski Valley, where the road ends. Drive to the highest public parking lot and park. You will see a Forest Service map and sign describing the area.

HIKING INSTRUCTIONS: A dirt road leads uphill out of the left corner of the parking lot (a sign on the road reads "No Parking"). Walk up it for about 50 yards to a signed trailhead indicating Bull of the Woods/Wheeler Peak Trail. The well-defined trail goes off to the left of the road in a generally northeasterly direction. There is a canyon on your right with a lovely stream. The first part of the trail is quite steep, winding through mixed conifers and aspen. Stay on the main trail. After about 10 minutes, and an elevation gain of 500 feet, you have hiked 0.3/mile. At this point the trail moderates. At 0.6/mile the trail jogs a bit to the left and then back to the right. Shortly after the jog, you cross the main stem of the stream (a very small feeder stream remains on your right).

After three-quarters of a mile and about 25 minutes, you'll see a sign on your left, facing away from you to the north. The sign indicates a trail leading off to the left: Long Canyon Trail/The Columbine-Twining Nat'l Rec Trail, indicating that Gold Hill is 4.5 miles away. Turn left and proceed up the Long Canyon Trail. The trail now contours along the right (east) side of Long Canyon in a northerly direction. The noise of the creek, down on the bottom of the canyon to your left, is very apparent. The trail "kisses" the creek from time to time as it climbs and becomes steeper.

One mile into the hike, the trail intersects a fence; there is an old gate on the ground. After about two miles (one hour) of hiking,

208

you will reach a beautiful meadow filled with wildflowers. You are now at 11,000 feet and a good rest area.

The trail now veers to the right to start ascending toward the top of the eastern ridge of Long Canyon. As you climb, you can look directly across the canyon to a beautiful high ridge with patches of snow even in summer and very evident avalanche chutes. Although this trail is a beautiful cross-country ski route, avalanche danger dictates against its use. Several years ago, an experienced skier was killed in an avalanche here while skiing alone.

Twenty minutes from the meadow, the trail levels out in another meadow, sparsely wooded with conifers and with good views of the high ridge. Soon the trail forks -- keep to the right! The main trail continues right and then makes an abrupt switchback to a southeasterly direction. Contour along the steep side of the ridge. Enjoy the beautiful views to the south. Look around at the scrubby trees, which show the strength of the wind up here. You can see some rare bristlecone pine. As the trail swings back from the southeast to a more easterly direction, you are almost at treeline and an altitude of 11,500 feet.

You will break out into a big meadow, which is actually a saddle of the ridge. There is a stone cairn on the edge of the meadow. Stand next to the cairn and look through the long axis of the meadow in a northerly direction. There's a whole series of cairns through this meadow, making it easier to find your way. You should see a trail sign, which you are approaching from the back, which indicates that you are intersecting the Gold Hill Trail. If you stand with your back against the front of the sign and look off to your left, you can see the next trail sign on the Gold Hill Trail. Head left for that sign. Note the old log cabin off to the right, which you will pass near on your return.

Walk through a beautiful high meadow above timberline. If you look to your right, you'll see some old mine tailings. The wind can be fierce from here all the way to Gold Hill -- over 50 miles per hour -- so be prepared.

The next trail marker is at an intersection with a faint trail that heads off to the right to Goose Creek and Goose Lake. The Gold Hill Trail goes uphill. You may have to slow your pace, since you're at an altitude with increasingly less oxygen. From this intersection, keep your eyes peeled for cairns marking the faint trail.

The next cairn has a trail marker on it for Lobo Peak (with a very faint trail heading left). You should be able to discern the Gold Hill trail heading up the rocky alpine tundra. The trail swings on up to the edge of the ridge, and for the first time you can see off to the east and northeast. You can see Goose Lake far below. The hill you've been looking at as you have climbed, probably thinking it is Gold Hill, is a little 12,000 foot bump to the south of Gold Hill. The trail contours around the southwest side of this bump and continues its steady climb to the real Gold Hill. On the summit of Gold Hill was once a USGS brass cap, but it appears that a cairn has been built over the cap. To the north you can see scars on the mountains from the mining activity between Questa and Red River, and beyond that the Latir Peaks.

Return down the trail the same way you came up. When you reach the big meadow in the saddle and the sign at the intersection of Long Canyon Trail and Gold Hill Trail, stay straight instead of turning right. You want to take this alternate route back, down the Gold Hill Trail to intersect Bull of the Woods Road and then back to the ski valley. It's easy to lose this trail at first because it's hard to see in the meadow. The trail heads down in an easterly-southeasterly direction. Look around the meadow for the trail leading into the trees. It is not cairned. As you head easterly, you should come to a little knoll with a dead log lying across your line of travel; you should then be able to see the trail approaching from your left and heading down into the trees. Turn right onto it.

Looking left, you can see the trail clearly going uphill to the old fallen log cabin.

At the right time of year, from the point where the return trail enters the woods all the way down to Bull of the Woods Pasture, this is an excellent mushrooming area. Through the end of June, you may encounter big snow drifts in the trees. The trail is blazed but you must be very observant if the trail is snow-covered. The trail winds in and out of the trees, and there are some spectacular views.

About 3 miles (an hour and a half) from Gold Hill, you intersect Bull of the Woods Road in Bull of the Woods Pasture. There is a nice pond which makes a good break spot. Head downhill on the road. (Uphill, the road goes to Bull of the Woods Mountain and the Wheeler Peak Ridge Trail.) The road has been closed for some years and is reverting to a trail since it has had no vehicular traffic. A little stream runs down the valley to your left. You'll note across the valley signs of mining activity: tailings piles and some stripped timber. After almost a mile, the road turns sharply left. Here is a small trail marker, a post with a very small sign saying "Twining" with an arrow pointing down a trail. Leave the road and follow the trail, which is well-defined with a small canyon to the left.

Soon you will find yourself at the intersection of the Long Canyon Trail and the trail you came up on from the ski valley, which makes a sharp right turn, downhill, with a small sign saying "Twining." Proceed down the trail you came up on, back to the parking lot.

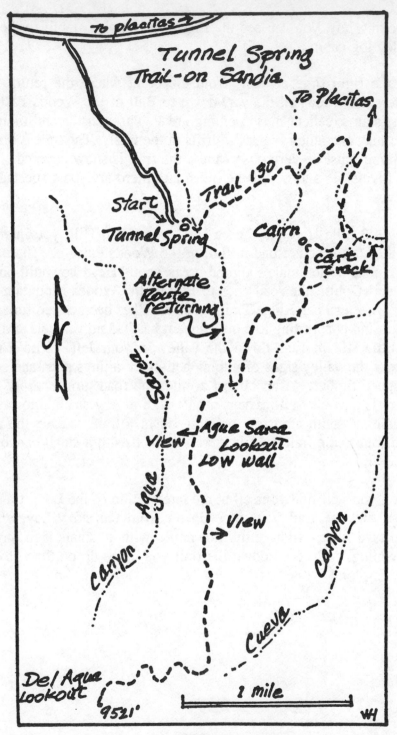

To placitas →

Tunnel Spring
Trail-on Sandia

To Placitas

Trail 130

Start

Tunnel Spring

Cairn

cart track

Alternate
Route
returning

N

Agua Sarca

Agua Sarca
Lookout
Low wall

VIEW

VIEW

Agua

Canyon

Cueva Canyon

Del Agua
Lookout

9521'

1 mile

WH

212

TUNNEL SPRING TRAIL TO DEL AGUA OVERLOOK
(In the Sandia Mountains)

by
Norma McCallan and Norbert Sperlich

Note: This is a revised version of the hike first suggested and written up by Polly Robertson in the earlier editions of this book.

U.S. GEOLOGICAL SURVEY MAP REQUIRED: Instead of the Placitas - 7.5 minute series, use the 'Sandia Mountain Wilderness' map, published by the US Forest Service and sold at the Forest Service office, 1220 St. Francis Drive, and outdoor stores.

SALIENT FEATURES: A hike into the Sandia Mountain Wilderness offering sweeping views. Lovely wildflowers. The walk from Tunnel Spring is all uphill on the north slope of Sandia; but it's ALL downhill returning. No water other than Tunnel Springs at the trailhead.

RATING: Moderate to strenuous, depending on distance travelled.

ROUND TRIP HIKING DISTANCE: 16 miles, but can be cut to any length you wish, as it is an "out and back" hike. If you take the alternate route down Del Orno Canyon returning, it is 14 miles.

APPROXIMATE ROUND TRIP HIKING TIME: 7-10 hours.

ALTITUDE RANGE: Highest point, 9640 feet; lowest point, 6400 feet; cumulative uphill hiking, 3240 feet.

SEASONAL CONSIDERATIONS: Best in spring or fall. Snow may linger in the upper reaches in early spring. Summer is hot.

ROUND TRIP DRIVING: 108 miles; about 2½ hours.

DRIVING DIRECTIONS: Take I-25 south toward Albuquerque. About 47 miles from Santa Fe, take Exit #242 towards Placitas. Make note of your odometer reading at the highway and go 5.2 miles east toward Placitas. After passing a street sign, "Puesta del Sol," on your right, look for the next dirt road to your right, marked "Tunnel Springs Road," with a group of mail and newspaper boxes. There is a small sign (FR #231) a few yards up this bumpy dirt road. Turn right here and drive 1.5 miles past several houses, bearing left if in doubt. You will pass the spring on your right gushing through a pipe behind a stone wall. The large parking area with toilet facilities is immediately beyond. Many people fill their water jugs at the spring.

HIKING INSTRUCTIONS: Trail #130 (North Crest Trail) starts next to an information board with a map. Crest Trail signs give the distance to Agua Sarca Overlook as 5 miles, Del Agua Overlook 8 miles and Sandia Crest 11 miles. You will start at 6400 feet. Agua Sarca Lookout is at about 7800 feet and Del Agua Lookout at 9640 feet. The time given on the sign to reach these spots is probably exaggerated for most experienced hikers. Trail #130 ultimately reaches Sandia Crest after 11 miles and continues to the southern end of the Sandias. Any part of this distance is a lovely walk.

Close to the trailhead, your trail crosses a drainage. There is a wooden sign, "Sandia Mountain Wilderness," at this point. Here, an unmarked trail goes to the right and up into Del Orno Canyon. You might choose to come down on this trail on the return trip.

For now, keep on straight ahead on Trail #130. To your left, in the distance, you can see Cabezon Peak, a volcanic neck, and closer by the Jemez Canyon reservoir and the fingerlike mesas of the San Felipe volcanic field. Next to your trail grows Mormon tea, a virtually leafless shrub with jointed stems.

Ignore two unmarked trails joining your trail from the left. The trail is a long, gentle traverse going northeasterly (toward Placitas) for about 1 mile, then it bears due south (right) and up Arroyo Colorado. You are hiking on grey limestone, deposited in an ocean 300 million years ago. Look for fossils! After you have followed the drainage for about 10 minutes, the trail levels out. There is a large slab of limestone in the middle of the trail which seems to be a marker for a faint trail coming in from the left. If you come back this way, keep the limestone slab on your right and stay to the left of the upcoming drainage.

The trail starts to climb again. About one hour into the hike, old cart tracks cross the trail at right angles. Five minutes later, another track approaches the trail from the left, runs parallel to the trail, then veers left again. Stay on the narrow trail to the right of this track. To the east, the Ortiz and San Pedro Mountains are coming into view now. Soon the trail turns west and takes you to the rim of Del Orno Canyon. Looking down the canyon, you can see your car. In the distance, to the west, appears Mount Taylor; to the north are the Jemez Mountains with Redondo Peak prominent.

For a while you will hike below the vertical cliffs that form the east rim of Del Orno Canyon. About 3.5 miles from the start of the hike, just before you come to the head of the canyon (where your trail crosses a drainage and turns sharply right), you will notice an unmarked trail that drops down to the right into the canyon. This is the start of the shorter alternate return route down the canyon which will save you about 2 miles. Note this junction

215

since you may want to return on it and it may be difficult to find on the way down.

About ten minutes after passing this trail junction, you will reach the east rim of Agua Sarca Canyon at the overlook, where there is a low stone wall on the right and expansive views to the west. It takes something under two hours to reach this point. This overlook makes an excellent place to stop for a break.

The trail now moves away from the edge, then returns briefly to the rim of Agua Sarca Canyon about half an hour further on. This overlook also offers great views. Soon the vegetation changes as piñon and juniper give way to dense scrub oak. Near some rock outcrops, where there is a sign for the "Peñasco Blanco" Trail (barely visible heading off to the left of the main trail), you can wiggle through the brush for a few feet to end up on a large flat rock which offers a great spot for lunch and a good turn-around point if you don't want to hike the entire distance. This "picnic rock" offers striking views to the east.

Keep on going straight ahead and up through the oak thicket. In late May, you should see lots of flowers during this section of the hike; the oak bushes will have leafed out and the gorgeous Fendler bushes should be in bloom. About half an hour past this trail junction, the trail returns briefly to the rim again, then turns left at a stone wall and keeps climbing in a southerly direction. The air is getting thinner and the oak bushes smaller, and you will have magnificent views to the north. In another half hour, the trail approaches the rim once more, leaves the oak behind, and goes into the fir trees. The trail makes a hairpin turn to the right and soon runs alongside the rocky rim, with great views to the west. There is no sign marking the Del Agua overlook; however, a stone bench close to the trail must be the place. Strong hikers can reach this point in four hours.

You may return to your car by the same route or take the shorter route previously mentioned. The shortcut saves you about 2 miles or one hour of hiking time. The trail descending through Del Orno Canyon is steep, a bit of a scramble, and rough in spots with a lot of loose rock, making for poor footing. Caution should be exercised while descending. Don't use this trail during or after heavy rains. It is bad enough in dry weather!

GLOSSARY

by Bill Chudd

Arroyo - A usually dry gully, at times containing a stream. After a rainstorm, or when there is a storm in nearby mountains, a dry arroyo may suddenly become a raging waterway.

Basalt - A dark igneous rock of volcanic origin, sometimes black and columnar.

Blaze - A mark on a tree made by chopping off a piece of bark. Blazes marking trails in the Santa Fe area generally consist of a short cut, with a longer cut below.

Blowhole - A hole through which gas or air can escape. Several deep pits in the Santa Fe area are commonly called blowholes, although they may or may not be the remains of ancient volcanic gas vents.

Borrego - A young lamb.

Cairn - A heap of stones; specifically, a pile of stones placed as a landmark, or to indicate a specific site or trail.

Caja del Rio - Box of the river. The Caja del Rio Canyon, popularly called Diablo Canyon, is a narrow, not a box, canyon.

Caldera - A large volcanic crater.

218

Camino - Road.

Cañada - Canyon, ravine.

Cerro - Hill.

Chamisa - The rabbitbrush, a ubiquitous grey-green bush whose odorous yellow flowers dominate the fall landscape of northern New Mexico.

Cholla - A tall spiny branching cactus with cylindrical stems.

Cryptogamic soil - A crusted, brown, fragile soil made up of mosses and lichens which takes many years to form.

Diablo Canyon - Devil Canyon (see Caja del Rio).

Divide - A ridge between two drainage areas.

Draw - A basin or ravine through which water drains.

Flume - An artificial channel, such as an inclined chute or trough, through which water is carried for irrigation or other purposes.

Frijoles - Beans (one of the crops cultivated by the ancient Indians in Frijoles Canyon).

Mesa - Spanish for "table." A small, high plateau with steep sides.

Moki stairway - Hand and toe holes dug by ancient Indians for scaling cliffs.

Petroglyph - A design cut or chipped into a rock face. Many interesting Indian petroglyphs may be seen in the Santa Fe area.

Piñon - The pinyon pine tree.

Puerto Nambé - Spanish for "Gateway to the Nambé."

Rio - River.

Rito - A small stream.

Saddle - A ridge between two peaks. Sometimes used loosely for any point where a trail or road tops a ridge.

Sangre de Cristo - Blood of Christ. The local mountain range was so named for the red color it reflects during some sunsets.

Santa Fe - Holy Faith. The full name of the city is "La Villa Real de la Santa Fé de San Francisco de Asis" - The Royal Village of the Holy Faith of St. Francis of Assisi.

Scat - Excrement, animal droppings.

Scramble - To climb or descend using hands as well as feet.

Scree - Same as talus.

Talus - A sloping bank of rocks at the base of a cliff.

Tarn - A high mountain lake or pond.

Tetilla - A small teat. Tetilla Peak was a landmark on the old Royal Road from Mexico, signaling the final approach to Santa Fe.

Tuff - A porous volcanic rock formed from compacted ash.

Viga - An exposed roof beam. (Originally a beam with which grapes or olives were pressed.)

Yucca - A plant of the lily family with sharply pointed, sword-shaped leaves.

SUGGESTED READING

HIKING:

Evans, Harry. <u>50 Hikes in New Mexico</u>. 3d rev. ed. Pico Rivera, CA: Gem Guides Book Company, 1988.

Hill, Mike, ed. <u>Hikers and Climbers Guide to the Sandias</u>. 3d rev. ed. Albuquerque: University of New Mexico Press, 1993.

Hoard, Dorothy. <u>A Guide to Bandelier National Monument.</u>. 3d ed. Los Alamos: Los Alamos Historical Society, 1989.

_____. <u>Los Alamos Outdoors</u>. 2d ed. Los Alamos: Los Alamos Historical Society, 1993.

Matthews, Kay. <u>Hiking Trails of the Sandia and Manzano Mountains</u>. Rev. ed. Santa Fe: Acequia Madre Press, 1991.

Montgomery, Arthur, and Sutherland, Patrick K. <u>Trail Guide to the Upper Pecos: Scenic Trips to the Geologic Past, No. 6</u>. 3d ed. Socorro: New Mexico Bureau of Mines & Mineral Resources, 1975.

Overhage, Carl. <u>Pecos Wilderness Trails for Day Walkers</u>. Santa Fe: William Gannon, 1984.

_____. <u>Six One-Day Walks in the Pecos Wilderness</u>. Rev. ed. Santa Fe: The Sunstone Press, 1984.

221

Parent, Laurence. The Hiker's Guide to New Mexico. Helena, MT: Falcon Press, 1991.

Pettitt, Roland A. Exploring the Jemez Country. 2d rev. ed., Dorothy Hoard, ed. Los Alamos: Los Alamos Historical Society, 1990.

Southwest Natural & Cultural Heritage Association. Trail Guide: Pecos Wilderness, Santa Fe National Forest. Albuquerque, 1991.

Sprenger, Joanne M. Trail Guide to the Las Vegas Area: The Sangre de Cristo Range of Northeastern New Mexico. Las Vegas, NM, 1987.

Ungnade, Herbert E. Guide to the New Mexico Mountains. 2d rev. ed. Albuquerque: University of New Mexico Press, 1972.

WILDLIFE:

Bull, John, and Bull, Edith. Birds of North America, Western Region: The Quick Identification Guide for All Bird-watchers. New York: Macmillan, 1989.

Cockrum, E. Lendell. Mammals of the Southwest. Reprint of 1982 edition, Books on Demand.

Findley, James S. The Natural History of New Mexican Mammals. New Mexico Natural History Series. Albuquerque: University of New Mexico Press, 1987.

MacCarter, Jane S. New Mexico Wildlife Viewing Guide. Helena, MT: Falcon Press, 1994.

Olaus, Murie J. A Field Guide to Animal Tracks. 2d ed. The Peterson Field Guide Series. Boston: Houghton Mifflin, 1975.

Peterson, Roger Tory. _A Field Guide to Western Birds_. 3d ed. The Peterson Field Guide Series. Boston: Houghton Mifflin, 1990.

Robbins, Chandler S., et al. _Birds of North America: A Guide to Field Identification_. Rev. ed. New York: Western Publishing Company, [no date].

Scott, Shirley L., ed. _Field Guide to the Birds of North America_. Washington, DC: National Geographic Society, 1987.

GEOLOGY:

Baldwin, Brewster, and Kottlowski, Frank E. _Santa Fe: Scenic Trips to the Geologic Past, No. 1_. 2d ed. Socorro: New Mexico Bureau of Mines and Mineral Resources, 1968.

Christiansen, Paige W., and Kottlowski, Frank E. _Mosaic of New Mexico's Scenery, Rocks and History: Scenic Trips to the Geologic Past, No. 8_. 3d ed. Socorro: New Mexico Bureau of Mines & Mineral Resources, 1972.

Kues, Barry S. _Fossils of New Mexico_. New Mexico Natural History Series. Albuquerque: University of New Mexico, 1982.

Muehlberger, W.R., and Muehlberger, Sally. _Española-Chama-Taos: A Climb Through Time: Scenic Trips to the Geologic Past, No. 13_. Socorro: New Mexico Bureau of Mines & Mineral Resources, 1982.

Thompson, Ida. _The Audubon Society Field Guide to North American Fossils_. New York: Knopf, 1982.

223

MUSHROOMS:

Lincoff, Gary H. The Audubon Society Field Guide to North American Mushrooms. New York: Knopf, 1981.

Smith, Alexander H. A Field Guide to Western Mushrooms. Ann Arbor: University of Michigan, 1975.

TREES AND SHRUBS:

Elmore, Francis H., and Janish, Jeanne R. Shrubs and Trees of the Southwest Uplands. 2d ed. Popular Series, No. 19. Tucson: Southwest Parks & Monuments Association, 1976.

Lamb, Samuel H. Woody Plants of the Southwest. Santa Fe: The Sunstone Press, 1977.

Little, Elbert L. The Audubon Society Field Guide to North American Trees, Western Region. New York: Knopf, 1988.

Whitney, Stephen. Western Forests. The Audubon Society Nature Guides. New York: Alfred A. Knopf, 1985.

WILDFLOWERS:

Arnberger, Leslie P. Flowers of the Southwest Mountains. Rev. ed. Globe, AZ: Southwest Parks and Monuments Association, 1983.

Dodge, Natt N., and Janish, Jeanne R. Flowers of the Southwest Deserts. Rev. ed. Globe, AZ: Southwest Parks & Monuments Association, 1985.

Foxx, Teralene S., and Hoard, Dorothy. Flowers of the Southwest Forests and Woodlands. Los Alamos: Los Alamos Historical Society, 1984.

Ivey, Robert DeWitt. Flowering Plants of New Mexico. 2d ed. Albuquerque, 1986.

Martin, William C., and Hutchins, Charles R. Fall Wildflowers of New Mexico. The New Mexico Natural History Series. Albuquerque: University of New Mexico Press, 1988.

_____. Spring Wildflowers of New Mexico. The New Mexico Natural History Series. Albuquerque: University of New Mexico Press, 1984.

_____. Summer Wildflowers of New Mexico. The New Mexico Natural History Series. Albuquerque: University of New Mexico Press, 1986.

Niehaus, Theodore F., et al. A Field Guide to Southwestern and Texas Wildflowers. The Peterson Field Guide Series. Boston: Houghton Mifflin, 1984.

Patraw, Pauline M. Flowers of the Southwest Mesas. Popular Series, No. 5. Globe, AZ: Southwest Parks & Monuments Association, 1977.

Porsild, A. E. Rocky Mountain Wildflowers. Chicago: University of Chicago Press, 1987.

Spellenberg, Richard. The Audubon Society Field Guide to North American Wildflowers, Western Region. New York: Knopf, 1979.

Tierney, Gail D. and Hughes, Phyllis. Roadside Plants of Northern New Mexico. Santa Fe: Lightning Tree Press, 1983.

Weber, William A. Rocky Mountain Flora. 5th ed. Boulder: University Press of Colorado, 1976.

MISCELLANEOUS:

Auerbach, Phil S. Medicine for the Outdoors: A Guide to Emergency Medical Procedures and First Aid. Rev. ed. Boston: Little, Brown, 1991.

Barker, Elliot S. Beatty's Cabin: Adventures in the High Country. Santa Fe: William Gannon, 1977.

DeBuys, William. Enchantment and Exploitation: the Life and Hard Times of a New Mexico Mountain Range. Albuquerque: University of New Mexico Press, 1985.

Kjellstrom, Bjorn. Be Expert with Map and Compass: The Orienteering Handbook. Rev. ed. New York: Macmillan, 1976.

Pearce, T. M., ed. New Mexico Place Names: A Geographical Dictionary. Albuquerque: University of New Mexico, 1965.

Wilkerson, James A., ed. Medicine for Mountaineering and Other Wilderness Activities. 4th ed. Seattle: Mountaineers Books, 1985.

Note: Some of the books listed above may be out of print, but will probably be available from libraries.

INDEX OF HIKES